What people are saying about

On a Common Culture

An elegant and significant contribution to cultural studies, informed by a much more pluralistic and wider field of theory, which includes Richard Hoggart, George Orwell and Matthew Arnold.

The argument here has the authority and importance of Hoggart's *The Uses of Literacy*: it's an intelligent and enlightening exploration of the uses of culture.

Tim Crook, Emeritus Professor, Media, Communications and Cultural Studies, Goldsmiths, University of London

On a Common Culture

The Idea of a Shared National Culture

On a Common Culture

The Idea of a Shared National Culture

Brian Russell Graham

Winchester, UK
Washington, USA

JOHN HUNT PUBLISHING

First published by Zero Books, 2022
Zero Books is an imprint of John Hunt Publishing Ltd., No. 3 East St., Alresford,
Hampshire SO24 9EE, UK
office@jhpbooks.com
www.johnhuntpublishing.com
www.zero-books.net

For distributor details and how to order please visit the 'Ordering' section on our website.

Text copyright: Brian Russell Graham 2021

ISBN: 978 1 78904 832 2
978 1 78904 833 9 (ebook)
Library of Congress Control Number: 2021930342

A CIP catalogue record for this book is available from the British Library.

Design: Stuart Davies

UK: Printed and bound by CPI Group (UK) Ltd, Croydon, CR0 4YY
Printed in North America by CPI GPS partners

We operate a distinctive and ethical publishing philosophy in
all areas of our business, from our global network of authors to
production and worldwide distribution.

To my wife, Margherita.

Contents

Preface

National identity and cultural equality are two highly significant themes in current debates inside and outside of academia. This study re-introduces the idea of common culture to the debate. Common culture, it is argued, is classless or egalitarian culture; it helps bring about cultural equality. Of course, when common culture was spoken of in a UK context a few decades ago, the culture in question was not simply egalitarian; it was also decidedly 'British', or simply 'English', and therefore both egalitarian and indigenous. F.R. Leavis, for example, speaks of how the highly educated and less well-off both enjoyed Shakespeare in Elizabethan times. England possessed a 'Genuinely national culture' (1933: 216), argues Leavis. Taking its cue from the Leavises, in this study, common culture is viewed as a font of national identity as well as a source of greater cultural equality. With regards to the former, it will emerge that common culture should be *comprehensively* national – the definition of a common culture should include as many local cultures as possible.

The two outcomes of common culture are highly desirable goals. We tend to think of cultural inequality as a gateway to other inequalities in society today. Greater cultural equality, then, is a crucial goal. National identity might be even more important for us. Ours is a time of astonishing polarization and fragmentation in the UK today, but national identity can generate social unity. We can never unite around class or identity politics or any other 'divider'; only the nation provides us with a focus we might all feasibly unite around.

The political Right defends national identity today; the academic Left champions the kind of equality in question. As a study which supports both goals, albeit through approaches distinct from those advanced by Left and Right, this volume

1

aims to simultaneously promote one goal of the Left and one of the Right. Left and Right, however, are interwoven in what follows. It is an *inclusive* national identity that is spoken of; and, with respect to the second goal, my argumentation is *traditional* in its acceptance of value judgements when discussing how to generate cultural equality.

Advancing ideas about common culture, my book also issues challenges to other trends in contemporary thought. With respect to common culture as national culture, it offers resistance to what I call hard-line multiculturalism, along with associated trends, namely identity politics and post-national cosmopolitanism, as well as a trend in the humanities to focus on the global or transnational (at the expense of the national). With respect to common culture as egalitarian culture, it offers resistance to what has been (and must be) called cultural populism. My study, then, offers resistance to both elite and populist tendencies in society today.

In connection with common culture and national identity, what follows is a study of the integration which is crucial to citizenship. Says Goodhart, 'For integration to have any meaning it must require participation in the mainstream in at least one big area of life – neighbourhood, or workplace, or leisure time (perhaps sports or hobbies)' (2013: 72). In what follows, I focus on leisure as a means of integration. To participate in common culture is to participate in a kind of mainstream; common culture participation, therefore, represents a form of integration.

It is also a study partly based upon the idea of what Appiah calls the 'liberal state' (2018: 103). As Appiah suggests, that state is founded on something as fragile as 'general willingness' (ibid.). 'What makes "us" a people', observes Appiah, 'ultimately, is a commitment to governing a common life *together*' (2018: 102). Of course, what I say about UK common culture will partly fall on unreceptive ears: plenty of Scots and Welsh people don't want to participate in British common culture. However, even here I hope what follows will have relevance. The ideas in this book might be used to evolve an understanding of common culture in a broad range of independent and potentially-independent countries.

The subtitle of a recent publication reminds us that today universities are hell-bent on convincing us that 'everything is about' gender, race and identity concerns more generally. This book bucks that trend to a significant extent. Chapter 2 creates a specific domain for considerations of gender and race, but in what follows those concerns play second fiddle to concerns which are more important in this specific context, namely social class and region or locale.

Much of the work done on common culture today is Marxist. In that kind of work, common culture is defined in terms of common consumption, but also common ownership:

> The idea of the common as it has been recently revived by Marxist scholars points not only at the participatory aspect of cultural production but also collective ownership of cultural resources (Dyer-Witheford 2010: 82; Hardt and Negri 2009; Harvey 2012: 73). Nick Dyer-Witheford stresses that commons are shared among collectivities: "The notion of a commodity, a good produced for sale, presupposes private owners between whom this exchange occurs. The notion of the common presupposes collectivities – associations and assemblies – within which sharing is organized" (2010: 82). Using Williams' (1989: 36) description of a common culture and these recent debates on cultural commons, we can thus identify two main aspects of a common culture: common participation and common ownership. (Sandoval 2014: 74)

My discussion belongs to a different background. Of course, we have little in the way of non-Marxist discussions of common culture – after the work of the Leavises, the trail goes rather cold. My study seeks to advance the non-Marxist tradition. It is rooted in the work of Richard Hoggart and Northrop Frye.

Neither Frye nor Hoggart is the first name that comes to mind when we think of common culture. There may be no reference to common culture in Frye's *oeuvre*, and Hoggart observes that the idea is more important to Raymond Williams (Corner 1991: 150). But this study reveals that the two are first-class sources when it comes to taking the discussion about such culture forward in a particular way. Hoggart's ideas about the importance of value judgements when dealing with culture are central to the first three chapters. Additionally, his vision of public service broadcasting informs chapter 5. Frye is an even more fundamental source for this study. The introductory chapter introduces his diagrammatic understanding of the levels of culture before turning to his definition of leisure. Chapter 2 makes use of Frye's notion of how national cultures comprise a multiplicity of local cultures, and chapters 2 and 3 incorporate Frye's ideas about how leisure is an activity which demands something along the lines of a form of high seriousness. Chapter 4 turns to Frye's ideas on literature, while chapter 5 opens with a discussion of both Frye and Hoggart. And chapter 6 is mainly about Frye's take on our fascination with culture containing portrayals of violence, although it does justice to Hoggart's earlier contribution to that topic, as well as George Orwell's still earlier commentary on brutalist entertainment.

This combination of influences takes us back to the combination of Left and Right floated a moment ago. Charlie Ellis has written persuasively of Hoggart's 'left conservatism' (207-209: 2008), which Hoggart shares with figures such as George Orwell and Bernard Crick (both of whom I also refer to in what follows). (For a full account of left-conservatism, see Eric Kaufman's 'The Rebirth of the Left-Conservative Tradition'.) My own monograph about Frye, *The Necessary Unity of Opposites*, deals with how he tries to move beyond Left and Right in his thinking. Most significantly, because it relies so heavily on Frye's reading of Matthew Arnold, what follows is characterized by a degree of sympathy for the mix of politics Frye ascribes to Arnold's writings and might be considered somewhat 'Arnoldian'. (Hoggart is also an Arnoldian, of course.) Arnold is enormously sensitive to the partiality of the politics of each of the social classes, his own included, and, in one reading of Arnold, the politics of each class is unredeemable. But, in Frye's view, Arnold rehearses how we might combine political sympathies which might seem mutually exclusive: the liberal, the social democratic and conservative. This theme is addressed in some detail in chapter 3. Interestingly, this combination of viewpoints is one which was vaunted by American sociologist Daniel Bell; and, more recently, David Goodhart, with Bell in mind, has labelled such hybrid politics 'postliberalism', suggesting they are the politics of a 'hidden majority' (2014: 52). In what follows, however, this viewpoint amounts to the simple notion that the ideal is that everyone in society is a producer, that everyone enjoys the kind of freedom that stems from taking leisure time seriously, and that that freedom is a *shared* freedom which unites us.

The ideal volume dealing with the idea of a common culture would be one which, at the very least, went through suitable theories of all the different arts, with important chapters on music, film, newspapers, etc., as well as other pastimes, including the various types of digital communication which we dedicate so much time to. In the end, most pages of that volume remain blank pages, as my contributions are modest. In addition to my more theoretical material, I will speak of just two specific areas: literature, on the one hand, and broadcasting (radio and television), on the other. The chosen foci speak to my own limited expertise, but they point the way forward, and my hope is that scholars in other fields may respond to the challenge and supplement what I say here with theories of common culture in the context of other areas. To that end, I have appended a 'Call for Contributions' for a future volume comprising a more comprehensive account of what common culture in the UK means in relation to a broader range of arts. In connection with the more general and abstract material, it is also hoped that this book will spur studies of common culture in other countries.

But if the ideal volume is beyond reach for now, this study is nonetheless written in what might be considered a utopian mode. It deals with the desirable or ideal, with what is possible if not probable. With Frye as a main source, this is an inevitability. His own writings are characterized by the same idiom. 'The Utopian writer', Frye comments, quite clearly reflecting on his own work to an extent, 'looks at his own society first and tries to see what, for his purposes, its significant elements are. The Utopia itself shows what society would be like if those elements were fully developed' (2009a: 192).

In what follows, I draw on earlier publications in which I ventured onto this territory. The idea that our response to common culture must be active and engaged, discussed in chapters 2 and 3, was first explored in 'Northrop Frye on Leisure as Activity', *Academic Quarter*, 11, Summer, 2015. Chapter 4 draws heavily on 'The Anti-Elitist Nature of Northrop Frye's Conceptions of Highbrow and Popular Literature', *Philologie Im Netz*, 84, 2018. I first broached the subject of chapter 5 in an article entitled 'Frye and Hoggart on Film and TV' published in *Hamilton Arts & Letters*, 7.2, 2015. And chapter 6 represents a reworking of the theme discussed in 'Northrop Frye and the *Opposition* between Popular Literature and Bestsellers', *Academic Quarter*, 7, Winter, 2013.

The development of common culture would amount to a change to the culture of our culture. To say that the way we consume culture is also cultural may sound confusing, but a moment's reflection confirms cultural factors determine how we enjoy culture. How much culture we consume, which culture we focus upon, when we enjoy culture: all of these can be construed as questions about our culture of culture, which sits alongside our culture of travel, culture of child-rearing and so on. This study advocates change to that culture. It is partly addressed to those who have significant decision-making power: the leaders of cultural institutions, members of education authorities, teachers designing curricula, and so on. But it is also addressed to the common reader. While recognizing that important structural issues get in the way of the evolution of common culture, we should not forget the individual at the centre of such concerns. This study is predicated on the idea that, even at an individual level, one can choose to embrace common culture as it is defined in the following chapters.

Introduction

Although the benefits offered by culture are legion, two benefits generate an enormous amount of interest today. First, some culture is national culture, and national culture provides us with national identity. Second, culture more generally offers us cultural capital: each one of us has a 'stock' of cultural experiences indicative of our taste, which can be considered a type of capital. With respect to national identity, in his 'Levels of Cultural Identity', Frye offers a three-level understanding of culture:

> On an elementary level there is culture in the sense of custom or lifestyle: the distinctive way that people eat, dress, talk, marry, play games, produce goods, and the like...Then there is a middle level of cultural identity, which is the product of tradition and history, and consists of the distinctive political, economic, religious, and other institutions that shape a nation's life and give direction to the main currents of its ideology...Finally, there is an upper level of culture as the product of a nation's specialized creative powers. (2003b: 639-640)

Frye suggests that the middle level is not the place to look for 'cultural symbols'. 'Those', he observes, 'come from either the lifestyle level or the creative level' (2003b: 640). When we speak of a person's culture, often it is 'capital' belonging to these two levels that we have in mind. If we adopt this way of thinking about culture, the picture that emerges is one in which each person possesses a certain amount of cultural capital (derived from different levels of culture), some of which is national and some of which originates in other countries. National identity is tied in with the former; a person's cultural capital involves both categories.

Of course, there is another side to these benefits: the two features speak to two problems connected to the effects of culture. Our lives have been centred on what in two different contexts we speak of as 'dominant culture', and that culture has two negative effects. In as much as the dominant culture is national culture it produces *exclusive* national identities. In another respect, dominant culture (the combination of national and foreign) produces cultural inequality in terms of capital; some enjoy dominant culture, while others limit themselves to other types of culture which are deemed subordinate.

This study deals with what can be called common culture. All upper level, along with a modest amount of elementary culture, is my focus. More or less, my theme is what Frye has in mind when he speaks of leisure, a point I shall return to presently. The following chapters explore the notion that common culture provides us with a partial solution to the aforementioned challenges. Common culture generates an inclusive national identity. Additionally, common culture can help generate cultural equality – not full cultural equality, but it can make a significant dent in cultural inequality.

Of course, my idea is not to prescribe a cultural diet of nothing but domestic culture. Such a diet would mean *assimilation* for minorities in societies, where my interest is common culture as a force for integration. Besides, we all need to supplement our enjoyment of common culture with an appreciation of the culture of other countries. This is axiomatic, but two particular reasons are especially apposite. One is that cultural inequality is generated not simply by our differing patterns of consumption of national culture, but by our differing patterns of consumption of culture generally.

If I may approach the second reason in a slightly roundabout way, the present study is certainly not intended as yet another volume touting the all-importance of an identity type which sets us apart from people in other 'groups'. Rather, in spite of its interest in national cultures, it is animated by a sense of the importance of our ultimately not being culturally segregated, nationally or internationally. My own conclusion about primary identity flies in the face of the conclusion emerging from political philosophies such as multiculturalism and nationalism. Anthony Kronman speaks powerfully of primary identity when he says:

> To our other identities, with their more restricted spheres of attachment, globalization adds our membership in an ecuméne organized on the premise of a universal humanity that transcends all such attachments. And it demands that this last identity be accorded a decisive primacy over the others (familial, tribal, religious, even political) in the sense that its requirements are acknowledged to constrain theirs. (2007: 175-176)

Kronman, of course, is careful not to set up this type of identity as an identity which dissolves other identities:

> Its primacy is not eliminative. It does not require that these other identities be forgotten or abolished. (2007: 176)

Today's focus on identity typically places each of us in separate communities with distinct heritage backgrounds and, theoretically, little means of communication across cultural barriers. Personal development means nothing other than enhancing one's identity within one's societal group. That view of the world holds that an art work is not 'of' a community different from the one in which it originated. Instead, I subscribe to Frye's paradoxical notion that as we study literature and the other arts, we become increasingly aware of the fact that particularity and universality represent not a dichotomy but a fortunate unity, a point we shall return to. Given a modicum of openness, British culture holds enormous appeal for the citizens of other nations, and, conversely, the culture of other nations holds great appeal for UK citizens, which they often discover on a daily basis.

Second of all, then, we need to combine our enjoyment of common culture with the culture of other countries because everyone's culture must go beyond the national, even if the national is fundamental. This is less of a danger for members of minorities who combine their participation in domestic culture with ongoing enjoyment of the culture of earlier generations of their families. For the majorities, other cultures are crucial because the consumption of nothing but national culture results in hopeless parochialism – a parochialism which, given the universal qualities of the arts, is utterly unnecessary. And, hopefully, when we combine participation in other cultures with enjoyment of domestic culture, we affirm what Kronman refers to as 'universal humanity', even if we accept that nationhood and national culture are important parts of the whole.

Of course, the necessary engagement with other cultures shouldn't lead us to imagine that we can get away from our own common culture. Perhaps cultural equality could be established via the consumption of nothing but the common culture of other places. But that would leave everybody without national identity. It looks as though there is no getting away from domestic common culture. (A number of further questions are suggested by these observations. In chapter 3, we'll turn to Hoggart, as well as Anthony Kronman, once more, for further insights into this theme.)

To return to Frye's concept of leisure, which informs my argument, Frye employs an understanding of culture which is in part close to what the Leavises thought of as 'minority culture': serious literature, painting, music, etc., each of which suggests education. One might conclude that Frye is simply recycling outdated Arnoldian ideas about culture. But when referring to leisure, he is thinking of culture in the wider sense. He distinguishes between 'creative arts' (literature, music, painting, etc.) and 'communicating arts' (film, television, radio, newspapers, etc., but also advertising and propaganda) (2003a: 9). (These terms are employed throughout this study.) The Leavises strongly disfavour the latter: for them, such arts are a kind of anti-culture. (See Storey for a neat summary of the Leavises' attitude towards the communicative arts (2015: 25).) Frye is more nuanced in his assessment of those arts. Advertising and propaganda are indeed a kind of anti-culture, in his view: as we shall see in chapter 5, he calls them 'anti-arts' (2003a: 41). But the other communicating arts, he concludes, are a mixture of the shoddy and the genuine, and a responsible attitude to culture involves a painstaking separating of wheat from chaff.

Frye's definition of leisure is yet broader than this. Frye and Raymond Williams were contemporaries, and, although Williams did not influence Frye, Frye's understanding of culture is very nearly as all-encompassing as that of Williams (see Hamilton 1999). As we shall see, in addition to the arts, Frye has a wide range of leisure activities in mind when he thinks of culture, activities which also suggest the elementary level of identity: attending a sports event, going for a drive in the countryside, and so on.

Strikingly, Frye repeatedly returns to the identity of leisure and education in his work, and one could be forgiven for concluding that by expanding leisure to this extent he is stretching the identification of leisure and education to breaking point. Some of our cultural pursuits may seem distant from education; but Frye insists on the identification in as much as it is possible. 'Television, newspapers, films, are all educational agencies', he states in one piece (2002: 225). As we shall see, the final litmus test for Frye is not the leisure activity itself, but the attitude adopted towards that activity.

Contents

In chapter 1, 'National Identity and Cultural Inequality: Challenges in the United Kingdom Today', I address the issues connected to identity and inequality just spoken of. I first rehearse putative solutions promoted by various parties in public debates in the UK: hard-line multiculturalism as a solution to issues connected to identity, and the vanquishing of value judgements as a solution for cultural inequality. I then go through the inadequacy of these prescriptions, drawing mainly on the ideas of Jonathan Sacks, Larry Siedentop, David Goodhart, Eric Kaufman and Francis Fukuyama in relation to multiculturalism, and Richard Hoggart in relation to the abolition of value judgements in cultural matters. Chapter 1 concludes with a short account of the desirability of common culture in the United Kingdom. Common culture, it is argued, can produce national identity, and it may help to bring about cultural equality.

Chapter 2, 'Common Culture as National and Egalitarian Culture', which shifts the focus to a more general and abstract level, offers a definition of common culture. The definition is three-fold. I begin by addressing the necessity of our incorporating geographic diversity when dealing with common culture, after providing a sketch of what is meant by the term 'national culture'. I proceed by discussing the value of working with a four-level understanding of the arts in this context. Proceeding to one of my main points, I suggest that common-culture material comprises the kinds of national culture characteristic of the two middle strata of the schema. Adding one further characteristic to my definition of common culture, I turn to mental attitude. Common culture is about unity, and attitude to culture can prove as much of a divider as greatly diverging tastes can. This section starts out by focusing on the fact that two contrasting attitudes to culture prevail today. On the one hand, the attitude which turns to culture for distraction; on the other, the attitude which insists that culture requires concentration and discipline. Drawing on Frye, the chapter turns to his idea that it is of the utmost importance that we approach culture with responsibility and discipline, which leads to the conclusion that common culture also depends on the mental attitude characterized by those qualities. I bring the chapter to a conclusion by considering variations on national common culture, tied in with different kinds of social identities.

Chapter 3, 'Objections and Responses', rehearses possible critiques of the three main points to emerge from chapter 2, before offering defences of them. I rehearse the 'world literature and culture' critique of national culture, a cultural populist critique of value judgements about different kinds of popular culture, and a Bourdieu-type critique of the preference for leisure over distraction, before providing responses to those critiques. First, I argue that while the notion of world culture is appealing enough, it fails to discredit the business of enjoying and studying culture as national culture. When offering a defence of an anti-populist approach to culture, I consider some of Hoggart's other ideas. And when defending the idea of a disciplined approach to culture, I rely on Frye and his reading of Matthew Arnold's *Culture and Anarchy*.

In the remaining chapters, the focus shifts back to UK common culture. In theory, chapter 2 'tees up' three categories of more specific discussions: commentary about the nature of the national dimension of common culture in connection with specific areas of culture; discussions about what passes muster as common-culture material in the realms of specific arts; and considerations, in specific contexts, of the significance of the idea that our response to common culture should always be responsible and disciplined. Chapter 5 deals with common-culture material in one particular domain; chapter 6 turns to the kind of mental attitude we might adopt when enjoying a particular type of common culture; chapter 4 is mainly concerned with common-culture material, but it also gives consideration to our response to that material and what that response yields.

'Common-Culture British Literature', chapter 4, turns to the literary theory of Northrop Frye. It first establishes that Frye provides us with a four-level understanding of literature which is a match for the general theory set out in chapter 2. It then explores the notion that the British literature of the two middle strata might be construed as British common-culture literature. It first clarifies that the literature belonging to the lower of these two strata easily qualifies as common culture owing to the minimal demands it places on the reader. Proceeding to the upper-middle stratum, it invokes a notion first presented in chapter 2, namely the idea that, while some putative common-culture material is challenging, the material of the lower-middle stratum actually offers the kind of training necessary for the appreciation of more difficult material. The chapter explains Frye's idea that popular literature provides the reader with the training required for more challenging literary works, specifically the work construed as upper-middle stratum material in this chapter.

'Common-Culture British Broadcasting', chapter 5, performs the same operation in relation to broadcasting. Working with the ideas of Hoggart, this chapter goes through his account of a four-level understanding of broadcasting, where, again, the two middle strata get construed as British common-culture material. This chapter takes 'the long way round' to this conclusion. It begins with Frye's tripartite understanding of society spoken of in the final section of chapter 3 and proceeds to the subjects of advertising and propaganda. It then provides an account of the view of public service broadcasting shared by Frye and Hoggart before honing in on Hoggart's vaunting of Huw Wheldon's programming ideal, which provides us with a compelling definition of UK common-culture broadcasting.

In the final chapter, 'The Ethics of Melodrama and Common

Culture', I turn to a specific example of how mental attitude is important if we are to secure a common culture in the United Kingdom. Working once more with Frye's ideas, I discuss his sense that there are two ways of responding to melodrama (one appealing, one unappealing), be it in literature or on television. I provide an in-depth account of his thoughts on melodrama, which reaches the conclusion that the disciplined and responsible attitude involves our treating such fictional material as an ironic game. I bring the chapter to a conclusion by turning to the finale of season two of ITV's *Broadchurch*, discussing it as the kind of melodrama which, against the backdrop of a common culture, we must respond to with irony and detachment.

* * *

With respect to the UK dimension of my argument, it may be useful to provide a little more context. Bailey *et al* argue (with reference to broadcasting) that Hoggart advocates the steering of a course between 'the populist Scylla of "giving the public what it wants" and the autocratic Charybdis of "giving the public what they ought to have"' (2011: 145), which is a fine metaphor for the approach I wish to advance. In the twentieth century, public discussion of common culture swung from advocacy of an unequivocally high-culture notion of common culture to a populist one characterized by the idea that common culture may feasibly comprise nothing more than works of mass culture. The Leavises were two of the earliest advocates of a common culture in the United Kingdom. Arnold, of course, had spoken of the need to make high culture the culture of as many people as possible – 'We must have a broad basis, must have sweetness and light for as many as possible', he observes – and the Leavises adopted his cause as their own. The two fretted over the notion of the public having no culture but popular or mass culture, and their solution was specific mass education programmes designed to provide the public with access to minority culture. At century's end, Paul Willis, by contrast, argues that common culture is burgeoning everywhere in the United Kingdom; but the common culture in question is not based on high or 'official' culture – it doesn't even feature high culture. Common culture consists in the everyday productive use of the material of mass culture.

The distinction at stake is between creative and communicative arts. A common culture which balances creative and communicative arts is *always* the right solution. Such a compromise is suggestive of a social contract. To exclude the communicative arts *in toto* is to exclude from 'culture' an enormous amount of the most vital creative work produced in the modern world. Conversely, to exclude high culture from a putative common culture amounts to what Frye would call an 'anticultural' attitude. Either way, the development is suggestive less of a social contract than a putsch.

With reference to the kind of balance my own study seeks to champion, it could be argued 'We tried this before and it didn't work'. Willis himself neatly sums up an earlier middle-way attempt to create a common culture in the UK:

> In the phase of social reconstruction after the [Second World War], part of the welfare-capitalist pact was to widen out the appreciation and practice of the high arts from their traditional base in the leisured upper-middle class. The arts were part of the good things of life which were to be shared out more equally. As in other areas, the state was to be responsible for this sharing out. The formation of the Arts Council in 1945 and the BBC Third Programme in 1946 was to spearhead this democratization of the arts. (1990: 4)

While there is certainly some overlap between what happened then and what I am advocating, as will become increasingly clear, my conception of common culture is also distinct from this attempt. It might, however, fairly be construed as a new contribution to the kind of historic drive towards common culture alluded to here.

Part One

1. National Identity and Cultural Inequality: Challenges in the United Kingdom Today

An exclusive national identity; cultural inequality. What are the solutions to these challenges in the UK today? At the end of this chapter, I'll rehearse my general solution to these issues. But the bulk of this chapter is dedicated to our current catholicons: hard-line multiculturalism (hereafter sometimes referred to simply as 'multiculturalism') and the vanquishing of value judgements about culture.

Exclusive National Identity and A Way Forward

When we consider how identity in the UK evolved away from a historic exclusive national identity, one of the most significant developments is hard-line multiculturalism.

Multiculturalism was championed by the cultural Left of the late 1960s, but its roots have been traced back to Horace Kallen and Franz Boas in the Anglo-world (Goodhart, 2013: 175), and to a generation of anthropologists headed by Lévi-Strauss in France (Finkielkraut, 1988: 90). (The two streams are connected, of course: Boas influenced Lévi-Strauss, a friend. Poignantly, Boas died in Lévi-Strauss's arms.) From the point of view of that outlook, Western cultures are hegemonic. Essentially a tyrannical force in history, the most striking characteristic of each Western culture is supremacism: its malignity stems from its viewing non-Western civilizations as inferior. It is, in other words, hopelessly Eurocentric. In as much as it has minorities at home, they are treated as second-class citizens who are outside the indigenous culture.

Central to the way forward is the acceptance that all cultures are equal, and a consequent enhanced valorisation of cultures previously ignored, undervalued or debased. This development postdates decolonization, and so the main effects are related to the cultural life in Western nation states. The lot of minorities at home becomes the focus of attempts to improve society. In this reading, Western culture and each variation of it are examples of white culture, and so the imposition of that culture and national identity on minorities through integration has an unappealing racial dimension. Indeed, for multiculturalists, obligatory partial inculcation into the home culture is a form of racism.

Without necessarily tackling it directly or explicitly, this approach to society de-emphasizes the individual and stresses a specific type of group or identity politics. Fukuyama sums up the differences between two types of identity politics. Looking back to the 60s, when a rift emerged, he recalls how

> Each marginalized group had a choice of seeing itself in broader or narrower identity terms. It could demand society treat its members identically to the way that the dominant groups in society were treated, or it could assert a separate identity for its members and demand respect for them as different from the mainstream society (2019: 107).

It is clearly the latter kind of identity politics which is part and parcel of hard-line multiculturalism.

Amartya Sen has called this type of multiculturalism 'plural monoculturalism' (2006: 156). Paradoxically, against such a backdrop, cosmopolitanism also comes to the fore. All of our ills stem from nation states; a cosmopolitan future will be a time of peace, tolerance and cooperation.[1] The alternative identity is one which is outward looking and international: cosmopolitan identity is multinational, multifaith, multi-ethnic, etc. Multiculturalism is enthusiastically post-national in this regard. And such post-nationalism involves not just political structures – the nation state – but also culture: freeing one's identity from the confines of one's national culture is a moral act.

This hard-line point of view began to enjoy a significant cachet in the UK in the 80s. In Goodhart's history of multiculturalism in the UK, this kind of multiculturalism, 'separatist multiculturalism', supplanted the 'liberal multiculturalism' which had been dominant in the UK up till that time (2013: 170).[2] From this point of view, the United Kingdom is part of Western hegemony. British history is a history of nothing but slavery, discrimination, segregation, brutalism, and starvation of dominated peoples, and multiculturalism is the way forward for the country. Assimilation or even integration is a type of oppression in this setting. Malik suggests that this kind of UK multiculturalism emerged out of anti-racism, specifically the anti-racist attitude of the Greater London Council (GLC) in the late 80s (2012: 59). 'Racism', he observes, casting his mind back, 'now meant not the denial of equal rights but the denial of the right to be different' (2012: 59). The year 2000 saw the publication of the Parekh Report, an iteration of the main ideas of UK hard-line multiculturalism, which spoke of the country as a 'community of communities' (2000b: ix).[3] British culture and the British population in the year 2000 were a mismatch, owing to the 'whiteness' of British culture:

> Britishness, as much as Englishness, has systematic, largely unspoken, racial connotations. Whiteness nowhere features as an explicit condition of being British, but it is widely understood that Englishness, and therefore by extension Britishness, is racially coded. "There ain't no black in the Union Jack", it has been said. (2000b: 38)

Of course, in the UK context, integration might just as likely have charges relating to chauvinism levelled against it. After all, from one point of view, integration amounts to adopting Englishness, Britishness being a thinly-veiled variation on that national identity. In proportion as hard-line multiculturalism began to organize life in the UK, alternative identities started to become more and more important.[4] To take one example, over the course of the nineties and the first decade of this century, Scots increasingly saw themselves as Scottish rather than British, when compelled to pick just one identity. In the words of the *British Social Attitudes* survey

> British identity clearly plays second fiddle to Scottish identity north of the border. Forced to choose a single identity, at most only around one in five say that they are British, while typically around three-quarters or so indicate that they are Scottish. (BSA 30, 2013)

Hard-line multiculturalism found itself in the doghouse from early in the new century.[5] Over most of the past two decades, the emphasis has been on integration without assimilation, where the emphasis is on civic identity. Another narrative, of course, suggests that, in the form of Black Lives Matter, hard-line multiculturalism is making a comeback today.[6] There is certainly some truth to this, but it is also the case that hard-line multiculturalism never went away. No doubt a significant amount of British life has been lived according to the norms and values of multiculturalism over the course of these decades. Indeed, Goodhart reminds us of new multiculturalist initiatives which postdate the twilight of multiculturalism: he mentions the opening of more faith schools and the passing of the religious hatred bill, before alluding to New Labour's wariness over fully supporting personal autonomy and free speech when they ran up against cultural sensitivities (2013: 225-226). And hard-line multiculturalism clearly has always retained advocates, especially in academia. For its advocates, for whom national identity is politically unappealing, multiculturalism remains the solution. In many younger advocates, the support for it can seem rather ahistorical. Not every supporter seems conversant with the history of the failures of hard-line multiculturalism laid out in the accounts of commentators such as Goodhart and Sacks.

To turn to a slowly evolving development which predates today's resistance to the idea of a cultural mainstream (although it shares its outlook), one of the clearest manifestations of hard-line multiculturalism is work being done in humanities departments on canons. Humanities departments make a significant impact on national culture and identity; and many scholars have been working against national identity for decades. To limit this discussion to the scope of one art, from the Leavises in their day, to Jonathan Sacks in ours, the literary canon has been seen as a font of national identity. Much of today's scholarship in this field amounts to an all-out assault on canon and therefore national identity. Inspired by multiculturalism, academic campaigners demand separate canons tied in with other identities. In the process, former national identity gets demoted or abolished, while other identities proliferate. On library shelves, volumes dealing with the Scottish canon sit beside studies of the black British canon, and so on.

Critique of Multiculturalism and Affiliated Trends

There is obviously much that is valid in the foregoing critique, but the proposed solution, hard-line multiculturalism, can be critiqued root and branch.[7] To begin with cosmopolitanism, cosmopolitanism would be fine if cosmopolitans were right, and the nation state were a thing of the past, but nation states remain crucial. Apologists for cosmopolitanism undervalue nation states to an extraordinary degree. In his recent *Identity*, Francis Fukuyama suggests that the nation state offers six 'goods'. First, it offers physical security (2019: 128-129). Second, the nation state is tied in with the quality of government (2019: 129). Third, it facilitates economic development (2019: 129-130). Fourth, it provides a 'wide radius of trust' (2019: 130). Fifth, it can maintain social safety nets (ibid.). And sixth, it makes liberal democracy possible (2019: 130-131).

A multiculturalist might conceivably accept this point but fall back on the notion that all cultures are equal, that integration is incompatible with the dignity of the members of groups and potentially racist in nature, and that for these reasons national identity is a discredited idea. But those points may also be challenged.

To begin with the notion that we should abolish national identity on the grounds of equality, it is important to understand the extent to which opponents of hard-line multiculturalism insist on the superiority of their own national cultures. Importantly, what gets vaunted in such defences of national culture is the cultural 'content' of what Frye thinks of as the middle level of culture, where institutions and values are most important. Kronman – approaching these issues from a US perspective – emphasizes the superiority of Western institutions (Kronman 2007: 172-173). In a UK context, Sacks and Goodhart, again with the middle level of culture in mind, boldly vaunt the values of 'liberalism' (Sacks, 2007: 18-19; Goodhart, 2013: 198-209).

Beyond that, the desire to preserve national culture need not have anything to do with the notion that one culture is better than another. With respect to the top and bottom levels of culture, the relative value of a particular national culture is potentially irrelevant. We may invest in such a culture, not because of some putative superiority, but purely on the grounds that national identity generates the social unity which is the antidote for polarization and fragmentation. Here we proceed on the basis of the fact that a society will have one culture and not another, and that for that reason its culture is *the* culture which can offer society particular benefits. Hence, the interest in national culture amounts to both a preference for the national middle level of culture and an acceptance of the national culture characteristic of the other two levels. And such a position is perfectly defensible.

Moreover, despite its emphasis on equality, multiculturalism is far from egalitarian, argue its critics. Says Sacks:

> It began as a commitment to value all cultures. Then it became valuing all cultures equally, a completely different proposition. Then it became valuing all cultures except your own. That is when it becomes pathological. (2007: 178)

Eric Kaufman provides us with further insight into this view in his recent *Whiteshift* – which also helps us to understand how multiculturalism can entail compulsory cosmopolitanism. Tracing the cultural Left's attitude to culture back to Randolph Bourne, Kaufman explains that multiculturalism not only encourages the maintenance and flourishing of minority identities in multicultural societies, but also the obligatory adoption on the part of majorities of cosmopolitanism – cosmopolitanism without cultural appropriation, in fact (2019: 341), which he sees as 'asymmetrical multiculturalism' (2019: 53). There is, then, little that is egalitarian about this prescription.

What of integration? Are there grounds for suggesting that even integration is oppressive? I'll return to the idea that integration might be chauvinistic later in this chapter. The notion that integration is a racist policy which diminishes the dignity of members of minorities is unconvincing. The idea that British culture is white culture, which lies behind the sense that integration is oppressive, is entirely bogus. At first such a perspective seems merely reductionist. Adopt another perspective and not only does a different profile emerge, but British culture also emerges as diverse.[8] But, on closer examination, it emerges that the viewpoint relies heavily on sleight-of-hand. Such argumentation boils down to something along the lines of, 'The "authors" of British culture have mostly been white people, therefore British culture is not the culture *of* non-white people'. Two points are clearly getting conflated in this statement: one, that British culture has been mostly produced *by* white people, and, second, that British culture is (therefore) exclusively *for* white people. The first is true enough (although less so with time), the second is false, and the conflation of the two is mischief.[9] We should not fail to notice the unusual overlap between left-wing radicals and right-wing extremists here. Both parties reject the idea that the British heritage is for members of non-white minorities. That should tell the radical Left something, but it seems unwilling to learn.

Also of interest is the more radical critique of identity politics, which suggests that a focus on the individual remains superior to group or identity politics. Siedentop suggests that the change can be understood in terms of two types of pluralism.[10] Drawing on Isaiah Berlin, he argues that 'One is a vision of social groups or cultures, each defined by and expressing its own values. The other is a vision of individuals choosing to pursue different values within a framework of law which protects individual freedom but also sets clear limits to such freedom' (2001: 201). Siedentop provides us with a defence of the kind of pluralism focused on the individual, along with a striking critique of the kind predicated on groups. Ultimately, it may be the case, Siedentop suggests, that the liberties of the two pluralisms prove incompatible:

The liberty of groups is not the same as the liberty of individuals. Respecting the beliefs and practices of a particular group, if that is understood as ruling out any interference in their ways, can indeed be described as respecting the "liberty" of that group. But that liberty may

26

involve an assault on or suppression of individual liberty (2001: 204).[11]

In terms of its effects, hard-line multiculturalism is also disastrous. Such 'plural monoculturalism' brings about a society which can only be more internally divided. A society such as the United Kingdom can be divided between Left and Right. Multiculturalism emphasizes further oppositions, which means that society becomes even more fragmented. Jonathan Sacks has spoken of the multicultural society as the 'hotel society', which is characterized by *de facto* segregation. 'The danger is', argues Sacks, 'that it turns society into a series of non-intercommunicating rooms' (2007: 16). Similarly, Malik has argued that multiculturalism in the United Kingdom has made the country 'more tribal' (2012: 68). Of course, in the UK, such critiques were first floated by Goodhart, who as early as 2004 had started to draw our attention to the fact that multiculturalism was trading solidarity for diversity.

To return to the humanities, from this point of view, of course, a proliferation of canons is not a thing to devoutly wish for; it is simply part of the means whereby we become an aggregate of different groups, not really living together in a national society at all. A fair amount of today's work on the canon represents a moderate, revisionist reconsidering of the canon, which opens it up to the writers who were undervalued or ignored in the past – many of whom are women, writers of colour, working-class writers, and so on.[12] This is obviously compatible with social unity; the proliferation of canons is not.

Emerging, then, out of the response to hard-line multiculturalism is a sense that, contrary to the cosmopolitan view, the nation state remains a vital unit of governance and culture today. In spite of the partial appeal of seeing cultures as equal to one another, the idea of national culture proves defensible. The critique of integration informed by multiculturalism is riddled with issues. The abandonment of the focus on the individual is a thoroughly retrograde step: the identity politics characterizing multiculturalism comes with a number of losses. And multiculturalism brings about an entirely undesirable social fragmentation, in which national identity gets lost.

Cultural Inequality and a Way Forward

Because culture represents a kind of capital, and because some kinds of capital are viewed as legitimate and therefore dominant, culture entails cultural inequality in the UK today as well. The researchers behind 'The Great British Class Survey', who share their results in *Social Class in the 21ˢᵗ Century*, discovered that the cultural life of UK citizens is divided between the privileged and the disadvantaged.[13] Their approach is two-fold. In the first instance, their focus is taste and participation. (Work in this area distinguishes between taste and participation. One can have a taste for westerns, but going to the cinema to see a western is participation.) In this regard, the authors draw our attention to a significant cultural divide between those with most income and education and those with far less, which can be understood in terms of cultural engagement and disengagement. On the one hand, one group likes fish and chips, eats out rarely, doesn't go to restaurants, doesn't like pop music, generally abstains from high culture, and so on, while a second group goes to the theatre, goes to the opera, ballet and classical music concerts, as well as museums and galleries, etc. (Savage *et al*, 2015: 104). (The approach of the researchers is to identify these 'consumption groups' first and then find out if the consumption groups are matches for social class groupings, which they prove to be.) That gulf may leave some room for an area of overlap, an embryonic common culture, if you will, but any such area is presumably very limited in extent.

Second, the researchers incorporate *attitudes* to cultural

consumption. In their view, it is also possible to discern a contrast between how people in the UK enjoy culture. On the one hand, the researchers note the prevalence of the view that 'one should have to "work at" appreciating culture, and that through carrying out this aesthetic labour it was possible to reach a higher level of appreciation' (2015: 119). This approach contrasts with respondents for whom 'cultural enjoyment was not something that needed labour or detachment, or which required a display of judgement' (ibid.).

Of course, a division by itself does not point to cultural inequality. Cultural equality results from value judgements being attached to a division. And in the view of these authors that is exactly what has happened. With respect to the activity cluster featuring going to the opera, ballet and classical music, etc., connected to the more well-heeled, the authors speak of how the dominant activities are 'more socially approved of – more legitimate…indicating the subtle pressures and assumptions at work' (2015: 105). And the same holds for attitude to culture or 'way of seeing'. Seeing culture in terms of effort and discipline, they argue, 'is important because it can be directed, implicitly or explicitly, against those who are less well-off and who have less formal education' (2015: 119). Snobbery is getting reconfigured, they suggest:

> Snobbery is therefore being redrawn alongside cultural capital itself. As forms of culture which used to be restricted to the educated middle classes actually filter down to a wider section of the population, the dividing lines are being redrawn so that it is *how* specific cultural activities are enjoyed which matters. It is now a badge of honour for the well educated to *refrain* from being overtly "snobby", and distinctions are more subtle – but all the more powerful for this. (2015: 121)

A great many scholars have a pronounced interest in a quick-fix cure for cultural inequality. What is proposed is a kind of revolution in how we evaluate cultural preference. The principal change ushered in by this revolution involves our abandoning value judgements about the enjoyment of levels of culture, especially lowbrow culture. Such judgements represent 'symbolic violence', and should be avoided at all costs. The result of this simple gesture might prove significant. Through the simple abolition of value judgements about cultural consumption we might abolish cultural inequality. No common culture is required.

The disestablishment of value judgements is also a portent of further change in Marxist academic circles influenced by Bourdieu. Here, conjoined to the injunction that we abandon value judgements to bring in cultural equality is a sense of the towering significance of cultural inequality. A great many of today's commentators are Marxists who are of the view that the tackling of inequality in the culture domain may well be of full revolutionary significance. Such commentators work against the backdrop of the kind of thinking which argues that we must be cognizant of different types of capital if we are to understand and challenge power. Power is a matter of the simultaneous holding of different, interconnected types of capital, of which cultural capital is of great importance. Because power depends on the possession of different types of connected capital, beginning to undo cultural inequality may be of revolutionary significance.

The revolution in question has been floated as a solution for cultural inequality in the UK, too. Indeed, a version of it is implicit in *Social Class in the 21st Century*, even if the authors voice four reservations about the Bourdieu paradigm (2015: 101-102). Implicit in what they say – indeed in what has been included here – is a judgement about judgements, a meta-value judgement, as it were, which conveys the sense that the real problem is value judgements about culture *in toto*. Get rid of value judgements and cultural equality may burgeon.

Critique of The Revolution

Of course, this way of thinking about culture emerged out of the same crucible of ideas as multiculturalism did. Referencing Bourdieu amongst others, Finkielkraut explains that

> Under the impact of the anti-colonialist struggle the most influential and daring sociologists of the 1960s combined the Marxist approach with the anthropological. They pronounced that modern society itself is divided into classes, each endowed with a distinctive symbolic universe…of these cultures one is to be recognised as legitimate. But beware of appearances, the sociologist warned. The position of the dominant culture was to be explained by the dominant position of the class whose specific situation it expressed. Intrinsic superiority, either in what the class produced or in its values, had nothing to do with it. The dominated classes experienced a humiliation analogous in principle and in its effects to that which the great European powers had inflicted on their colonial peoples. (1988: 60-61)

The real problem is the putative solution, namely the abolition of value judgements. This idea about cultural equality enjoys an enviable cachet in the humanities today, but it may be subjected to robust and effective criticisms. A critique of this attitude to culture and society might begin by pointing out that the revolution in question is decidedly paradoxical in that it is a revolution in which, in the first instance, cultural egalitarianism operates hand in glove with capitalism. A clear outcome of this revolution is that sanctions on cultural consumption stop altogether, and such a discontinuation of sanctions is good for business. Some Marxist theories (those of the Frankfurt school), it is true, bewail the nature of 'the culture industry', while others emphasize the insidious ideological power of popular culture. But other egalitarian accounts of culture – the Bourdieuian, for example – throw the emphasis onto how value judgements about culture are coded attacks on the people who enjoy said culture. Addressing the consumer of culture, capitalism says, 'Don't feel guilty about enjoying this culture. It is material which culturally is not beneath you. All that matters is that you can afford it – that you are on the right economic level'. Certain kinds of cultural egalitarians say, 'All value judgements about culture are thinly-veiled attacks on people who enjoy that culture'. Thus, a pact of sorts holds. Value judgements might discourage the purchase and enjoyment of some marketable culture on the grounds of quality. But the abolition of value judgements ushers in a culture of culture in which everything can be sold because no reservations can be made about the consumption of any type of culture. Advocates of the revolution in question have an answer to this, of course. Once again, as this revolution spreads, hierarchies are challenged and power structures begin to give way. But the complicity between the two worldviews can only give an observer of such a development pause for thought.

In his writings, Frye repeatedly emphasizes the importance of the independence of the leisure sector, a theme we shall return to in chapter 5. There is always a danger that leisure gets co-opted by the economy or government or both. The 'revolution' in question is strongly suggestive of a situation in which the leisure sector is fully integrated into industry or the economy, so that all that matters is marketability, a solution which Frye associates with the political Right (2003a: 50).

Various commentators have pointed out that such a development is also populist in a number of respects. In the first place, it is suggestive of cultural populism. Populism means giving the public what they want. Bad political populism refers to selling the public a bill of goods and 'giving them what they want' in that context. Cultural populism parallels bad political populism, one might argue: bad political populism tries to convince us that a programme bereft of real policies amounts to a panacea, and cultural populism aims to persuade us that consumption bereft of 'Culture' represents *bona fide* cultural participation. McGuigan speaks of the cultural populism which characterizes our times, defining it as 'the intellectual assumption, made by some students of popular culture, that the symbolic practices of ordinary people are more important analytically and politically than Culture with a capital C' (1992: 4). And, of course, cultural studies is the embodiment of such cultural populism, as McGuigan and others have contended. Within the world of media, it is represented by the populist attitude to broadcasting and journalism associated with the Rupert Murdoch dynasty.

But the development in question is also undoubtedly suggestive of a larger populist development involving the putative 'democratic' superiority of the market compared with high politics. Following on from the work of McChesney (1996), American commentator Thomas Frank has called this phenomenon 'market populism'. As Frank explains, this type of populism not only exposes culture to market forces, it also advances the idea that the market sector is superior to political democracy in terms of democratic representation. Looking back to the dawn of this phenomenon, Frank fleshes out its assumptions:

Markets expressed the popular will more articulately and more meaningfully than did mere elections. Markets conferred democratic legitimacy; markets were a friend of the little guy; markets brought down the pompous and the snooty; markets gave us what we wanted; markets looked out for our interests. (2002: xiv)

Hoggart is the critic *par excellence* of this tendency. In chapter 3, we will turn to some of his most perspicacious criticisms of cultural populism, but we might profitably consider one or two of his observations at this juncture as well. In one study, he laments the fact that judgements of cultural value are no longer fashionable:

Why are so many people so violently disinclined to admit any differences in the value of different works of art; or between human choices as to activities? This is one of the most revealing of our cultural hang-ups...They avoid any vertical judgments in favour of the endlessly horizontal... The suggestion that there is a difference in quality between *North and South* and *The Ragged Trousered Philanthropist* or *Brother to the Ox*, valuable though Tressell's and Kitchen's books are, will produce letters accusing you of a narrow, highbrow vision, socially motivated snobbishness and an out-of-date clinging to a received order you do not have the guts to question. (1995: 57-58)

Hoggart's comments on how cultural studies evolved makes it clear he blames some academics and the development of cultural studies for this cultural dead-end (1995: 174), which aligns him with McGuigan and others. But it is clear that he has all manner of influential bodies in mind when speaking of this phenomenon: the media (broadcasters and newspapers), the Arts Council, and so on. And, of course, in his view it is advertisers, the 'mass persuaders', who are largely responsible for this new norm.

In Hoggart's view, we discover the full wrongheadedness of abolishing value judgements if we look further into what transpires when we proceed along those lines. Of course, the simple elimination of value judgements in connection with culture might leave us in a situation in which everyone enjoys the culture they like, undisturbed by censure. If one person likes Russian classics and another Tom Clancy, both may confidently turn to the literature of their choice, secure in the knowledge that no one will suggest a vertical relation between their tastes. But in Hoggart's view, the situation in not quite as benign as that. The current cultural situation goes well beyond the sanctions of those who would rid our cultural life of value judgements. Culture is dominated by something along the lines of a parody of proper judgements of quality. Recent *faux* cultural egalitarianism passes itself off as a manifestation of a genuine desire to 'level' society. But, in Hoggart's view, that conceals another drive: specifically, a desire for a type of culture to be recognized as superior. This putative cultural democracy is actually characterized by a strong admixture of what Fukuyama dubs 'megalothymia' ([1992] 2012: 182). The new norm passes itself off as democratic, but we should be careful, says Hoggart:

> This "democratic" attitude can produce a sort of totalitarianism of its own, a collective and inevitably lowbrow world in which all are expected to toe the line, to go the way that the world is going…Dismantling old snobberies of social class is fine; to fall into the explicit rejection of any worth whilst at the same time encouraging a new range of differences and snobberies, based on the contrast between a populist mass and a meritocratic minority; this is a very bad bargain. (1995: 50-51)

Of course, what Hoggart is driving at is not a revolution in which working-class culture, as defined by thinkers such as Williams or Hoggart himself, becomes the new dominant taste. It is an 'egalitarian' revolution which is capitalist and, in the cultural domain, populist – where whatever sells is sold to those who have the income, without the interference of value judgements:

…the only standard is the echo back. If the roar of the crowd comes back, that is success, and so unanswerably right and good. This is the numbers game, a substitute for judgments, the refusal to tangle with "better" and so "worse". (1995: 10)

Ultimately, we are left with conformity and a pseudo-common culture: 'Few will stand out against the insistent half-hidden appeal to common taste not always because they are afraid but sometimes because they do not wish to appear impolite by going against the tide which is apparently carrying with it so many millions of "ordinary decent folk"' (2004: 49).[14]

Interestingly, this critique of cultural populism ties in with a different view of equalities across different sectors. As we have already seen, some Marxist commentators emphasize how value judgements establish cultural hierarchies which are causally related to other inequalities. By contrast, commentator Bernard Crick argues that cultural populism results in a diminished demand for other equalities. Culture *is* 'upstream' to socio-economic realities, but not as Bourdieuians would suggest. In an article titled 'Big Brother Belittled', Crick suggests that the cultural life of Airstrip One is close in spirit to the cultural life of the UK in the year 2000. An enormous amount of cultural life involves purely commercial culture:

Orwell's picture of Big Brother's strategy…brings us close to the world of sitcoms, game shows and the prize inanities of the Big Brother show. The party made no attempt to activate the proles in support of the regime. They are simply depoliticised by cultural debasement, dumbed down, kept from even thinking of demanding fair shares. The party looks after the proles by producing for them rubbishy newspapers, containing almost nothing except sport, crime and astrology; sensational five-cent novelettes; films oozing with sex; and sentimental songs which are composed entirely by mechanical means on a special kind of kaleidoscope known as a versificator. There was even a whole sub-section "Pornosoc" engaged in producing the lowest kinds of pornography. (Crick 2000)

Crick provides us with a fine account of how cultural inequality props up other inequalities in such a society:

Orwell was deadly serious in arguing that capitalism, faced with a largely literate and free electorate, could only by means of cultural debasement maintain a class system so grossly unequal and inequitable. (ibid.)

On Common Culture

It would be hard to find an apologist for the old-fashioned attitude to national identity and cultural capital. The most hidebound approach to these matters would stick to the notion that British identity is the identity of the upper class only, and that it is actually a good thing for that class to have superior cultural capital. The ground we have shifted onto should be clear enough by now. A great many in academia promote the kind of society outlined above: a 'hotel society' (2007: 18) where all belong to groups, all groups live side by side and no value judgements about culture are aired by the 'culture of culture'. As I have clarified, the downsides to such a set-up are manifold. Such a set-up disestablishes a cultural mainstream, and results in cultural segregation. While it demotes national identity, it vaunts cosmopolitanism, even though that ideology may misjudge the importance of the nation state. It also gives identity politics a central role in national life, although, at least in certain forms, that understanding of society comes with significant drawbacks. And last, but not least, our cultural lives are left with little or no protection from the full impact of market forces.

The mooted solutions are riddled with problems; but the larger issues at stake are *bona fide* concerns. What, then, is the alternative to these solutions considered? A good number of alternatives emerge out of considerations of cultural identity rather than cultural capital. Sacks himself is an advocate of a type of identity already alluded to: civic identity. Closer to today, Fukuyama speaks of the desirability of national identities, which he ties in with both citizenship and public virtues. (In a discussion more limited to the US context, Lilla also throws the emphasis onto citizenship.[15]) At the very least, however, these ideas badly need to be supplemented by other ideas about national identity more tied in with everyday culture.

Kaufman himself is an advocate of a kind of symmetrical multiculturalism. Like Kaufman I want to bring in the other levels of culture, but I would like to go in a different direction from him.[16] (I'll return to Kaufman's thesis in the epilogue.)

Before we proceed to an alternative solution to these issues, we might return to the exclusivity of national identity and the failings of hard-line multiculturalism. The push for inclusivity actually fails to adequately address important sources of dominant identity in the United Kingdom. The first is social class, which is emphasized in discussions of cultural capital but ignored to far too great an extent in the context of multiculturalism, even though it is obviously central to dominant identity in that domain. Speaking critically of the 'country house' kind of society, the society produced by dominant culture, Sacks observes that 'Britain's country house had more to do with class than race' (2007: 17).

The second is geographic. The multiculturalist critique draws our attention to Anglocentricity, but this aspect of dominant identity is not simply a matter of the dominance of England. It is also about 'locales'. As Robert Crawford argues in *Devolving English Literature*, the literary world in the United Kingdom has been dominated by London, or later, the 'London-

Oxbridge nexus' (1992: 13), and other locales have at least at times been marginalized as a result. The same is true of culture more generally. National identity will become less exclusive when our conception of it becomes far broader in terms of the culture of the localities of the whole country. It could be argued that all that is needed is a kind of 'national diversity', involving our paying equal attention to Scotland, Wales and Northern Ireland. But simply placing greater emphasis on the other three nations in a vague way would not solve the problem of exclusive identity. After all, in the process of tackling Anglocentricity in this way, we might simply set up a small number of additional cultural capitals. So, in Scotland a Glasgow-Edinburgh nexus might represent a challenge to Anglocentricity, and so on. That would do little to tackle exclusive national identity; the rest of Scotland, to stick with that nation, might easily be ignored, and dealing with Anglocentricity in this way would do nothing to integrate the rest of England either. Only by focusing on different locales can we fully decentralize culture and identity.

National identity can be exclusive because of the above-mentioned factors; additionally, cultural inequality is a social problem. The better solution to these challenges is represented by common culture, which might offer an alternative solution to the two problems in question. After all, a moment's reflection should confirm two things about common culture. The first is that it is cross-class. The second that it is fully diverse in terms of region or locale. And defined in this way, common culture presents a solution to the challenges we are dealing with. Because of its two features, the national identity stemming from common culture can only be inclusive. And because it is cross-class in nature, common culture can also help to generate cultural equality (without a reactionary abolition of value judgements). In this latter regard, common culture can help with further equalities. The significance in this new context of Crick's last observation is obvious enough: the creation of a not a matter of proceeding to the stage where the 'ethnicity of the culture' (the entirety of UK culture, past and present) and the contemporary ethnicity of the population become a match. We could only ever arrive at the stage where there is a match between the ethnicity of British culture and the ethnicity of the British population by badly skewing British culture: we would need to tilt it very aggressively towards the recent chapters of British culture.

Fortunately, there is no need for there to be a match between the ethnicity of, say, authors, on the one hand, and readers, on the other. As already suggested, all culture is for *all* nationals, and, needless to say, all common culture is for everyone, even if, from the point of view of one type of identity politics, such culture is (unhelpfully) deemed 'white culture'.

But what is common culture? In Part Three, we shall return to the specifically UK context. But first we might consider that question on a more general and abstract plane, where we may approach the issues in such a way that the conclusions are of relevance in the United Kingdom but also beyond.

Part Two

2. Common Culture as National and Egalitarian Culture

I

Let's turn first to the national dimension of common cultures. Common culture obviously can't be limited to the culture of one particular national locale. Culture generates national identity, and if the culture in question is limited to one place, national identity can only be twisted out of shape. You could argue that the culture of, say, the Western Isles can't possibly be part of the common culture of someone living in Sussex; but we need to recover a sense that it most certainly is. The culture of those islands is indeed part of the national cultural heritage of a person from the other end of the country.

Presently, I'll address the fact that common culture must incorporate the culture of as many areas of a country as can be justified – it must be comprehensively national. But first it is necessary to address the very idea of national culture. When considering the national character of common culture, we need to consider both upper-level activities (for example, enjoying a film produced in one's country) but also elementary level activities (say, attending a local sports event). But most of the difficulties arise when we focus on the upper level of culture, which, for that reason, must be our main focus. What is it that permits us to say that an artist or art work is 'national'?

Some readers would no doubt prefer to skip or eliminate the definition of national culture. They prefer the notion of an international cosmopolitan culture, which they, along with everyone else, have a stake in and can relate to. In academic circles, the preference for such a vision was brought about by what we might call the 'transnational turn'. (In the next chapter, we'll consider the issue of 'meaning' in relation to these considerations; here I'll limit the focus to the identity of writers and other artists.) In a world in which so many artists are migrant artists, perhaps it is best if we admit that the national boundaries they cross and re-cross are, in the end, irrelevant when we are speaking of the arts of today. Perhaps writers are residents of what Bill Ashcroft has called the 'transnation' (Ashcroft 2013: 13). Two phases of the arts in the twentieth century seem especially relevant here: modernism and post-colonialism. Bradbury says of modernist artists, 'frequently it is emigration or exile that makes for membership of the modern country of the arts, which has been travelled by many great writers – Joyce, Lawrence, Mann, Brecht, Auden, Nabokov...the writer himself becomes a member of a wandering, culturally inquisitive group – by enforced exile (like Nabokov after the Russian revolution) or by design or desire' (1976: 101). Emphasizing the difficulty of placing modernist writers in national contexts, Bradbury cites George Steiner, who speaks of 'the "unhoused" writer' (ibid.), whose relationship with language seems to disconnect him from home and put him at the centre of an intensely internationalized community (ibid.). Post-colonial literature, the second category which raises challenges regarding the integrity of the notion of the national writer, is also apposite. Numerous artists have moved from an ex-colony to countries such as France, the UK, the Netherlands, and so on, just as, say, Forster went to India in the colonial period. Adiche lives in the United States and Nigeria. Rushdie, as a child, came to England when he was 10-years-old and now lives in the United States. And so on. How are we to categorize such itinerant writers using only national categories?

The problem is that, viewed through the lens of the full history of culture, only a relatively small number of artists belong to this group. As Frye and Kundera both emphasize, to move from one place to another is a difficult transplant. Speaking of such a sojourn of the artist is fairly short-lived.

The attachment to locale may even be historic rather than contemporary with the period of creation. It is equally legitimate to discuss the work of an artist in his or her original national context, owing to a sense that, although an artist has left his or her country of origin, their country has not left them. No one would suggest that Stevenson ever ceased to be a Scottish writer owing to his extensive travels or his spending the last period of his life on Samoa.

Kundera's meditation on 'Emigration Arithmetic' offers illuminating observations about the identity of the émigré creator. His focus is the hybrid identities of so many of his favourite writers, but also the strong undercurrents which mean they remain writers belonging to their original national contexts, regardless of where they live. Conrad's Polishness comes out in his 'allergy' to Russian culture (1995: 93). Bohuslav Martinů lived in France, Switzerland and the United States, but always thought of himself as a Czech composer (ibid.). Witold Gombrowicz lived in France and Argentina but could only write in his native Polish (ibid.). Some of Nabokov's characters are recognizably Russian, Kundera tells us (1995: 94). Kazimierz Brandys moved to Paris in 1982 but wrote in Polish and worked with nothing but Polish themes (ibid.). Says Kundera, 'The adult years may be richer and more important for life and for creative activity both, but the subconscious, memory, language, all the understructure activity, are formed very early' (ibid.).

This is, of course, as liberal a conception of the national artist as possible, and it might be objected that it represents a rather rapacious attitude to culture. A critic of this liberal approach might bring up what we might call the Heaney Conundrum too: how should a scholar respond when a writer objects to a critical attachment to a particular national context?

If the attempt to integrate artists into a particular national context can be construed as rapacity, the tendency to hoard artists might just as easily be construed as cultural possessiveness, as well as cultural essentialism. No doubt it is beneficial if we resist the notion that an artist is the exclusive treasure of one particular national culture. It is clear enough that artists can be fairly adopted as national artists in both the locale s/he has migrated to and the place s/he has emigrated from, provided, we might add, recognizable elements of a national identity persist.

Divided communities present us with a significant challenge, but even here the best answer is probably a matter of accepting that a multiplicity of national contexts are entirely legitimate domains for the understanding and enjoyment of artists and their works. It is startling when an author, for example, rejects a specific national identity as an artist, but such contextualizations are probably not something an artist can control, just as artists are not authorities on the meaning of their works.

* * *

Once we have regained our confidence about the notion that it is legitimate to think of artists as national artists, we may proceed to a key dimension of the definition of common culture, alluded to earlier. On close inspection, we see that such common cultures consist of instances of culture which have *local* identities. If we insist on speaking of national identity, that does not mean that the nation's identity is uniform. National identity is comparable to the effect produced by the typical photographic mosaic. When we look into the detail, we see that it consists of numerous distinctive identities. At the same time, it is not simply a random aggregate of different images; from one point of view, they make up a whole which is of at least equal importance.[1]

In his discussion of national identity, focused mainly, but not exclusively, on Canadian identity, Frye models how we might profitably understand and speak of culture and identity in this way, which makes him an invaluable source. I started out with Frye's discussion of the three levels of culture, and proceeded to the point that national identity is tied in with the elementary and upper levels. Of course, no sooner has Frye made the point that national identity is bound up with those levels than he clarifies that, if we scrutinize any culture-produced national identity, what we find is that it consists of a multiplicity of different types of identities. Making the point by speaking of his own country, he says, 'Canada is the Switzerland of the twentieth century, surrounded by the great powers of the world and preserving its identity by having many identities' (2003b: 641). He then brilliantly conveys a sense of how the imagination and the arts are regional in a country such as Canada:

> An environment turned outward to the sea, like so much of Newfoundland, and one turned towards inland seas, like so much of the Maritimes, are an imaginative contrast: anyone who has been conditioned by one in his earliest years can hardly become conditioned by the other in the same way. Anyone brought up on the urban plain of southern Ontario or the gentle *pays* farmland along the south shore of the St Lawrence may become fascinated by the great sprawling wilderness of Northern Ontario or Ungava, may move there and live with its people and become accepted as one of them, but if he paints or writes about it he will paint or write as an imaginative foreigner. And what can there be in common between an imagination nurtured on the prairies, where it is a centre of consciousness diffusing itself over a vast flat expanse stretching to the remote horizon, and one nurtured in British Columbia, where it is in the midst of gigantic trees and mountains leaping into the sky all around it, and obliterating the horizon everywhere? (2003b: 413)

While this variegation is characteristic of Canada, he sees it

47

as typical of works of the imagination of all countries. Literature in the United States and the UK is similarly varied on account of its having a regional or local character (2003b: 412-413). Frye remarks that

> The question of identity is primarily a cultural and imaginative question, and there is always something vegetable about the imagination, something sharply limited in range. American writers are, as writers, not American: they are New Englanders, Mississippians, Middle Westerners, expatriates, and the like. Even in the much smaller British Isles we find few writers who are simply British: Hardy belongs to "Wessex", Dylan Thomas to South Wales, Beckett to the Dublin-Paris axis, and so on. Painters and composers deal with arts capable of a higher degree of abstraction, but even they are likely to have their roots in some very restricted coterie in Paris or New York. (2003b: 412-413)

Of course, the vision of the arts promoted in this kind of theory is one which has been suppressed by an overemphasis on putative cultural capitals. Common culture, then, also involves what has been called 'devolving' culture, so that we recover a more decentralized or polycentric account of national culture. It involves, for example, integrating marginal literature into our idea of British literature, the literary culture of the Orkney Islands (George Mackay Brown), the Isle of Lewis (Iain Crichton Smith), the north east (Lewis Grassic Gibbon) and other Scottish locales, for example.

The fashion today is to define the artists of a country through the categories of identity promulgated by identity politics: we speak of the British minority writers, British female painters, etc. Frye's approach doesn't exclude such considerations. He simply advises us to attend first to the specifics of the geographical identity of an artist – to disaggregate national artists, as it were – when we want to speak of American, UK, Canadian, etc. artists.

The reader might worry that if artistic endeavour has such a local character, it may fail to pass muster as national material. To be national surely means that everyone in the country can relate to an art work; but can they relate to it if it belongs to and is suggestive of a completely different locale? Moreover, from the start I have suggested that it should be possible for each of us to relate meaningfully to the culture of other places – we want to combine domestic common culture with the common culture of other nations. But now the relational challenge seems ever greater. How can I respond in a meaningful way to something in a little-known locale in a perhaps far-away land?

Frye's focus on the local, however, does not mean that every artist is hopelessly limited in his or her appeal. Quite the opposite. Indeed, he is typically at pains to stress the fact that particularity and universality represent not a dichotomy but a fortunate unity:

> There is a curious law in culture, at least literary culture, which says that the most specific settings have the best chance of becoming universal in their appeal. (2003b: 645)

Approaching the arts in this way, then, we should remain confident that, even if the arts emerge as more local than we might have assumed, we can rest assured that they will prove not just nationally but universally resonant.

II

In each case, common culture must be defined in connection with the full geographic diversity of the culture of the country. But not all of the culture of a place qualifies as common culture. Another consideration circumscribes what passes muster as part of the commons. While we need to be as inclusive as possible in relation to geography, we must be thoroughly discriminating when it comes to *strata*. Crucially, some strata of culture lie outside the realm of common culture.

Let's keep the focus on the arts and proceed by considering a diagrammatic understanding of the arts that is commonplace in our culture today. When dealing with some of the arts, it is customary enough to think in terms of a middle domain, where high and low meet and combine. By and large, this is part of the legacy of postmodernism in the arts. It is conventional to think in terms of modernism as a time when there was a gap between high culture and low culture, and postmodernism as a time when that gap was closed.

It is revealing to examine how critics demonstrate that the gap was closed. Sometimes the focus is on the consumer of culture – the gap was closed owing to a new openness on the part of the reader or listener. In her 'One culture and the new sensibility', Susan Sontag characterizes the new openness in a very memorable closing passage:

> From the vantage point of this new sensibility, the beauty of a machine or of the solution to a mathematical problem, of a painting by Jasper Johns or a film by Jean-Luc Godard, and of the personalities and music of the Beatles is equally accessible. (Sontag,1966: 304)

However, usually critics are interested in finding qualities in the cultural world which explain how the gap has been closed. Writing in 1997, Hunter and Kaye, using verbs like 'blur' and 'to be eroded', depict our cultural world as one in which no demarcation can be made. Our culture is much less hierarchical than before – it may even be thought of as a horizontal culture:

Growing numbers of adaptations of "classic" literature, novelisations of films and new media such as laser disks, CD-ROMSs and the Internet blur the lines between film and fiction, reader and author, spectator and participants as well as mass and elite culture. (Hunter and Kaye 1997: 2)

In this multimedia age, barriers are eroded between film and fiction and between elite and popular culture: director's cuts, never seen at the cinema, are now available on laser disk, including commentary with the film. Films like *Braveheart* (1995) spawn CD-ROM interactive adaptations, *Babylon 5* creator, J. Michael Straczynski, corresponds with fans on the Internet. (Hunter and Kaye 1997: 9-10)

All cultural phenomena are redeemed by this revolution and suddenly anything which might constitute 'pseudo-culture' simply vanishes from our view. Everything in our culture now possesses some value. Because the distinction between high and low fails, value is diffused throughout the cultural world, and nothing is untouched by the diffusion. Thus, Lawrence Alloway fondly remembers how

the area of contact was mass-produced urban culture: movies, advertising, and science fiction. We felt none of the dislike of commercial culture standard among most intellectuals, but accepted it as fact, discussed it in detail, and consumed it enthusiastically. (Storey 2015: 183)

The postmodernist outlook suggests we look at the cultural landscape differently from the modernists. They may have thought in terms of the palace of high art and the entertainment of the masses, but from the later twentieth-century perspective, mass culture is of enormous interest and undoubtedly valuable.

Although that diagrammatic understanding is common

enough, there is an alternative way of organizing the arts which is conventional, although our awareness of it is less developed. When dealing with culture, we may profitably work with a four-level understanding of the creative and communicating arts.

Discussions about postmodernism in the arts often posit a single intermediate middle category, where high and low meet and combine, but some commentaries suggest that there are good reasons for adopting a schema characterized by *two* middle strata. Two kinds of critical gesture are relevant to this understanding of the arts. Often a critic sets out to demonstrate that material belongs not to the top or bottom category but to one of the two middle categories. A highbrow work is shown to have popular features; conversely, a work of popular culture is discussed in terms of merits (intellectual, aesthetic, etc.) which allows us to conclude that we may justifiably view it more favourably than other works of popular or mass culture. Of particular interest to some critics, then, is the notion of a popular culture which is touched by the 'distinction' of high culture. Thus Louis Menand constructs the postmodernist moment in terms of the appearance of a popular culture which is sophisticated even though it is popular, his sweep including albums, novels, sitcoms, a music label, a musical, the work of a visual artist, and a magazine:

> Just up ahead…a different dispensation was poised to come into being. This was a culture of sophisticated entertainment that was neither avant-garde nor mass, that was commercial but had a bit of brow. This was the moment of *Sgt. Pepper's* and *Bonnie and Clyde, The Spy Who Came in from the Cold* and *All in the Family,* Motown and *Blonde on Blonde, Portnoy's Complaint* and *Hair,* Andy Warhol and *Rolling Stone.* (Menand 2011: xx)

At the same time, other critics take the other route,

approaching the highbrow's engagement with the popular. In 'Cross the Border – Close that Gap: Postmodernism', perhaps the most well-known discussion of the postmodern phenomenon, Fiedler suggests that the new generation of writers, the 'young Americans' of the time, embrace 'Pop forms'. Where Menand thinks of a popular culture which absorbs the sophistication of high culture, Fiedler records how serious writers adopted genre fiction:

> The forms of the novel which they prefer are...at the furthest possible remove from art and avant-garde, the greatest distance from inwardness, analysis and pretension; and, therefore, immune to lyricism, on the one hand, or righteousness social commentary, on the other. It is not compromise by the market-place they fear; on the contrary, they choose the genre most associated with exploitation by the mass media: notably, the Western, Science Fiction, and Pornography. (Fiedler 1972: 351)

We should not fail to see that when discussing culture in this manner, commentators are, through their combined efforts, not only helping us to understand that the middle domain may be twofold; they are also setting up a diagrammatic understanding in which there is a top category to which the popular is quite alien, and a bottom category which doesn't have much brow. The outline of a four-level schema is perceptible. And, in specific commentaries, we find critics working with such a schema – they also turn their attention to work which, it might be thought, is extraneous to the domains where high and low blend and combine. A filmmaker such as Peter Greenaway might impress us as an artist whose work lies outside such strata, in the top-most category. Not so, say some Greenaway scholars. 'While many Greenaway critics continue to accuse him of elitism and hostility towards mass culture, it must be noted that his pastiche borrowings are not limited to so-called high art but include contemporary forms of artistic expression deemed more "popular"' (2008: xx), claim Willoquet-Maricondi and Alemany-Galway. Similarly, we might have assumed that prime time, bums-on-seats entertainment of the *Who Wants to be a Millionaire?*-type would be stuck in the lowest category. Not so fast, says Television Studies scholar Matt Hill. The programme in question may be positively valued if approached through the framework of 'popular aesthetics', he argues (2005: 177).

More importantly, the objective of this critical culture, if I may call it that, is to uncover the interpenetration of high and low in the culture of periods other than the contemporary, so-called postmodern one – perhaps *all* periods except for one, about which I shall say something presently. In the chapter following this one, I will turn to Frye's account of English literature which argues not only that much Anglophone popular literature is of enormous cultural value, but also that most serious Anglophone literature is characterized by an affinity with the popular. The works of, say, Tolkien represent popular literature of considerable merit – indeed, his literary fiction is in the tradition of romance, which is usually popular and always of value. At the same time, serious literature, such as works of literary Romanticism, are characterized by the profound influence of the popular. William Blake is a popular writer, argues Frye.

The same argument can be made in relation to music: it may be that an enormous amount of our music heritage belongs to the two middle levels, too. There is little to surprise us in the notion that much popular music is of great cultural value, but it is still surprising to many that much of our highbrow music, 'art music' is the preferred term in the scholarship, has popular roots. But that is exactly what musicologists have demonstrated. In his *Roots of the Classical: The Popular Origins of Western Music* (2004), for example, Peter Van der Merwe argues that, over the course of the eighteenth and nineteenth centuries, different kinds of popular music provided inspiration for all kinds of art music. Semi-Oriental popular music, the waltz, the polka family (the contredanse, ecossaise, galop and others, as well as the polka), the nineteenth-century vernacular (dances, marches, and so on): classical music drew on all these popular forms, explains Van der Merwe – their impact can be discerned in everything from the 'Gypsy Rondo' of Haydn's Piano Trio in G to the prelude to Bizet's *Carmen*. The distinction between art music and popular music emerged in the nineteenth century, but nineteenth-century Romantic music is connected to the popular, nonetheless. Wagner, for example, absorbed the idiom of east European folk music through Liszt, explains Van der Merwe (2004: 366).[2]

In relation to this critical process, one or two areas prove more difficult for commentators to deal with in this way. In one respect, the top and bottom categories are suggestive of the modernist period, and the works of that period are the most difficult to construe along these lines. High modernism seems radically highbrow, and the popular material of the period can seem bereft of the ambition of the popular material of other times. But even here there is room for such social developments of culture. There is a history of changes in perception of the popular work of the modernist period. Raymond Borde and Etienne Chaumeton's work on *film noir* (1955) represents an example of criticism which fleshes out the artistic merit of a type of popular film of the later part of the period. More ambitiously, in his study of modernist art, historian Thomas Crow (1996) shows how, in the modernist period, avant-garde art and popular culture are characterized by deep-seated interdependence.[3]

Common Culture

On a more abstract level, the result of such critical endeavours is a schema running from the very highbrow at the top, all the way down to the most popular at the bottom. (See Figure 1.) What we have here is a vertical, although it is not exactly a vertical running from the most valuable to the least valuable. True: a value judgement separates the two lower domains from one another: the favoured popular has merits less in evidence in the disfavoured popular, although the latter is more commercially successful. And, for the best part, the two upper areas are characterized by more ambition if compared to the two lower, also suggestive of a value judgement. But the popular-highbrow is not aesthetically inferior to the top-most category. It simply has more in common with the popular. The vertical, then, is characterized by some value judgements but organized around the idea of 'brow': it runs from the most highbrow to the most lowbrow, although, in terms of brow, the difference between the two lower levels is fairly slight.

Strata
'Elite'
Highbrow and popular (the popular-highbrow)
The favoured popular
The disfavoured popular

Figure 1

The commentator whose work is closest to what I am outlining here is Jim Collins. In the introduction to *High-Pop*, Collins speaks of the 'desacralization of culture' (2002: 6) and 'transforming *Culture* into mass entertainment' (ibid.). What I am laying out is related to what Collins outlines, but it is also different. Collins thinks of two processes as episodes in a historical progression. He ties the former in with Pop Art and the latter with the High-Pop phenomenon, which is the focus of his (edited) volume. In connection with the former, my interest is in all manifestations of the favoured popular. In relation to the latter, my interest is narrower. Collins is interested in, for example, the process whereby we produce and broadcast lavish adaptations of nineteenth-century novels, thereby bringing aspects of the cultural heritage to the public.[4] My focus is on the idea that much high culture possesses popular features independent of transformations.

That said, what interests me about this schema and its features is identical to what interests Collins about Pop Art and High-Pop: it provides us with a framework which allows us to evolve new ideas about a common culture. The middle categories are to a significant extent our focus; together, they might be seen as the levels of the arts of a nation which represent common culture. The logic runs as follows. If highbrow material is also popular, it may emerge as the kind of material which is not just of interest to the high-status, but the less advantaged, too. On the level of the favoured popular, it appeals across classes as well. The fact that it is popular means that it speaks to people, but highbrows take it seriously because of its merits. Of course, I used a value judgement in connection with the two upper and two lowers levels. Following the logic of value judgements, we could find ourselves prescribing the culture of the upper levels. But when thinking of common culture, we ultimately need to shift our critical focus away from value judgements to something along the lines of *suitability*, which draws us away from top and bottom to the middle areas of the structure.

It could be objected that even if our patterns of consumption were to go in this direction, people's enjoyment of the outer (top and bottom) levels of culture might remain unchanged to an extent, and that, consequently, this culture might not pass the test for a common culture at all. For a culture to pass muster as a common culture, *all* consumption of national material would need to be limited to these middle levels. Otherwise, we have cultures, one of which, for all the overlap between it and other tastes, would be easily identifiable as the culture of the socially dominant. But this is an absolutist view, and perhaps it is unnecessary. We should say, rather, that there comes a point when so much national culture is shared that it is appropriate to speak of a common culture. Different groups in society go on enjoying some material from the top and bottom strata, but they also participate, much of the time, in the common culture.

Significantly, the same tension characterizes work about inequality and class-based tastes. While fleshing out the nature of such distinct tastes, contemporary commentators may concede that there is a limited area of commonality without retracting their main point about power and contrasting tastes. Bennett *et al* speak of how television watching, going to the cinema and reading a daily newspaper represent shared cultural practices (2009: 132). Conversely, while identifying a potential common culture we can acknowledge that different (class-based) groups also consume a limited amount of national culture extraneous to the common culture without invalidating the main observation.

Further Features of a Common Culture

What I am offering here might amount to no more than the first observations regarding a new definition of the arts dimension of common culture. No doubt all kinds of refinement need to be added to what I have outlined. New hierarchies can always emerge, even within an apparently democratic domain such as common culture, and we should be Argos-eyed about new hierarchies springing up, updating theory when necessary to forestall or extinguish such developments. Indeed, we need to add greater nuance to the schema right away. What we have is a vertical, running from the most highbrow to the most lowbrow. But if we want to map different types of arts, we will need to use a *sequence* of diagrams which occupy different vertical positions. Hoggart speaks of the need for different verticals when taxonomizing culture: 'The scales of value should run from the very top to the very bottom of what is offered at any time, in any genre; but some scales reach higher, and some lower than others' (2004: 60-61). The sequence of diagrams I have in mind offers something different. As already suggested, the organizing principle in what I am saying is 'brow'. But we need something along the lines of what Hoggart alludes to.

Two important observations suggest themselves. The disfavoured popular stratum of the communicative arts is more lowbrow than the corresponding stratum of the creative arts. And the two highbrow strata of the creative arts are more highbrow than the highbrow strata of newer communicative arts. Hence, some types of favoured popular involve more 'reaching down' on the part of the high-status; some types of popular-highbrow require even greater 'reaching up' on the part of those with less cultural training.

The first of these observations allows us to revisit and better define the kind of taste that Hoggart is concerned about; it is a taste for nothing other than communicative-arts bottom-stratum material, and some commentators have construed such taste as tantamount to an infantilization of culture (see Finkielkraut, 1988).

More importantly for this study, the second observation suggests a further characteristic of common culture. If the highbrow strata of the creative arts are more highbrow than the highbrow strata of newer communicative arts, then it is of the utmost importance that common culture involves the enjoyment of material from the middle strata of *both* creative and communicative arts. Quite clearly, if one variation of the common culture were to involve nothing but creative-arts, middle-strata material, while another involved only middle-strata material from newer arts, it would be easy to see that the common culture had come undone. It makes sense to assume that one might have a foot in the creative arts by virtue of the enjoyment of the middle strata of even a single art (say, music), rather than the whole panoply of conventional arts. An enjoyment of middle-strata music combined with a love of common-culture film, television programmes, etc. could be judged as participation in the common culture. Coming the other way, for there to be a common culture, highbrows need to have a foot in the newer arts, which, in practice, is less of a problem today.

Of course, the difficulty of highbrow creative-arts material for those with less 'cultural capital' is a formidable issue, and some cultural training is obviously necessary if such common culture is to be accessed. I will return to this concern in chapter 4, when I discuss literature, but at this stage, it is worth briefly pausing to consider this question on the more general and abstract level.

Another feature distinguishing the favoured from the disfavoured popular within the realm of the creative arts is that the former fosters what we might call *cultural mobility*. Again, Hoggart is our guide. It may well be that a person can proceed to the popular-highbrow creative arts through training that they acquire by means of experience of favoured-popular creative arts. This involves a rejection of the cultural mores of our time, entailing a certain amount of non-conformity. The cultural climate we glanced at in the first chapter is one which Hoggart associates with *the carousel*. Summing up the truisms of what he calls 'mass society', Hoggart suggests that it is asked of us that we accept

...that people cannot be mistaken, whatever they continue to accept, and that they should remain happily on...the carousel – no hint of any "onward and upward" progress in taste, from Pavarotti's selected arias to the whole of *Turandot*, only an endlessly level and circular ride...(2004: 52)

Hoggart contrasts the carousel with 'the escalator' (2004: 17). While acknowledging the fact that society primes only some for the escalator, he vaunts the importance of the escalator for all society: the kind of mobility he has in mind is clear in the above quotation. It will become clearer as we proceed how common culture, especially *vis-à-vis* the creative-arts area, relies on such cultural mobility. Of course, it will also become clear that there is no reason to stick to a national context when speaking of such mobility; common-culture material of another national culture might easily provide the training one needs for the popular-highbrow of one's own culture. We should also bear in mind that the mobility required to meaningfully enjoy a work belonging to one type of art may be acquired through another art – it may be that we acquire an ability to understand more complex literary works through our experience of favoured-popular film, for example.

III

The nature of common culture is becoming clearer: it amounts to middle-strata material tied in with different national locales, as well as other (national) culture belonging to the elementary level of culture. One further feature is of crucial importance, however. We also need to consider mental attitude to culture when discussing this subject. After all, common culture admits no divisions; and such is the transformatory power of mental attitude when approaching culture that without a shared mental attitude to match shared common-culture material, we will end up not with a common culture but separate cultures. If I have narrowed the focus to the arts, in this new context we must open it up again, so that it becomes leisure more generally. I'll approach that theme after having given some consideration to taste and participation.

Taste and Participation

We can imagine what a common-culture taste might look like. Let's imagine a person from the United Kingdom in his 40s who enjoys various types of culture. His culture includes enjoyment of foreign culture, but also a great deal of the kind of material that passes muster as middle strata UK culture. He likes a good amount of UK cinema which falls into these categories. He has access to the country's PSB channels as well as one streaming service, and likes one particular tabloid newspaper, although he prefers the better journalists who contribute to the paper. On top of these preferences, he supports a particular football team, and takes an interest in rugby when the Six Nations tournament comes around each year. He also happens to be a voracious reader, enjoying everything from Dickens to children's literature. Music doesn't play a big part in his life. Last of all, he likes short hikes: the countryside near to where he lives possesses a modest beauty.

Of course, he doesn't simply *like* this culture. He participates. He goes to the cinema, in addition to watching films at home with his partner and friends. He also spends a fair amount of time watching PSB channels and using his preferred streaming service, and he buys the newspaper and reads articles in it most days. He often watches sport on television, but five or six times a year he also goes to a game (football rather than rugby). He reads a lot of fiction and non-fiction, often using his local library. Sometimes he reads when out walking, which he does at least once a month.

One could sound an optimistic note about the potential for such a common culture to emerge. After all, the common-culture taste/participation that I am defining seems to be close to an 'omnivorous' type of taste/participation, and there has already been a movement of taste away from highbrow taste to omnivorous taste. Perhaps we are already half-way there. Of course, such taste/participation is typically seen as *dominant* taste/participation (Kern and Peterson 1996; Bennett *et al* 2009). But such taste/participation is only dominant for as long as the conditions which prevent the less well-off from embracing a similar pattern of taste/participation to a far greater extent persist. And the whole thrust of the present project is to suggest how progress can be made in this area.

Of course, the issue of common-culture infrastructure crops up when we begin to consider participation. Guy Standing has written persuasively of the decimation of the cultural commons in the UK over the past 4 decades. The 'erosion' affects public spaces, public architecture, public libraries, museums and art galleries, public theatre, the mass media and public art (2019: 229-254). Standing outlines a 'Charter of the Commons' which would restore the commons (cultural commons included) which needs to be in place for common life to flourish (2019: 349-356).

Additionally, when we shift from taste to participation, the issue of income rears its head. Earlier, I emphasized the idea that, on one level, culture is upstream to economic circumstances. But we must also concede that, in certain respects, the opposite is true. Up to a point, common culture participation might not depend on much money. People can watch common-culture television (on the PSB channels) and read common-culture literature without much expense, for example. But culture is also a matter of engaging in activities which cost more money – going to the cinema, for example – and so only a society where the less well-off still have sufficient disposable income and free time can ever hope to have a common culture in terms of participation.

Culture and Attitude

In connection with common culture, my greater interest is in attitude. In a situation in which everyone enjoyed common culture in terms of taste and participation, after a change in the culture of culture, as well as necessary changes to our economy, a distinction, effectively spoiling the emergent common culture, could nonetheless easily emerge. For there is also the question of the kind of attitude one adopts to culture. I outlined the cultural enjoyment of a hypothetical UK citizen a moment ago. Let's now work with two people, both of whom apparently participate in common culture in something like the manner I sketched. These two might adopt such different attitudes to the same material that no common culture would be shared by them. Perhaps one takes culture that bit more seriously than the other. He pays attention to details, looks things up, making sure he understands what he is reading or watching. Sometimes it seems as though he puts as much effort into culture as he puts into work. Our second man of culture is rather less serious and organized in his enjoyment of literature, film, etc. He often feels that, were he to take the programme he is watching or book he is reading seriously, it would quickly start to feel like hard work, but he doesn't, so he spares himself the bother. In his more unguarded moments, he jokingly confesses to enjoying 'gratuitous violence' in entertainment. Interestingly, unlike his friend, he is also wont to get carried away by certain TV dramas, especially crime drama. He takes a peculiar delight in the perpetrator getting his comeuppance.

Undoubtedly, our response to culture is a cloven response. We are all on a spectrum where our response varies from the serious-minded to the flippant. And this has implications for common culture. Even if people in the country were to fully unite around taste and participation, no common culture would come into existence: response would create at least two cultures. I have already rejected the Bourdieu-type solution for this division – the simple obviation of value judgements. Another solution must be found. Clearly, if we are to make headway with what a common culture in the UK and elsewhere might look like, we need to address the issue of attitude. A common culture can only come about when a common attitude is brought to bear on common-culture taste/participation.

Frye on Mental Attitude

The most illuminating theorist of attitude to culture is (once again) Northrop Frye. Frye's idea is that everyone in society, in as much as they can, should enjoy leisure and avoid what he calls 'distraction' or, more damningly, 'boredom'. As we shall see, leisure requires 'discipline and responsibility' (2003a: 49-50) rather than distraction. (Of course, this helps us to understand his identification of leisure with education: 'leisure activity which is not sheer idleness or distraction depends on some acquired skill, and the acquiring and practice of that skill is a mode of education', he observes (2003a: 50).) Here we see a significant overlap between Frye and Leavis: Leavis also insists that mass culture is often characterized by 'distraction' (Leavis and Thompson 1977: 100). In the following description, 'leisure' refers not to the cultural activities themselves, but the attitude we take to them. Frye provides us with snapshots of an important opposition:

> The difference between leisure and distraction or boredom is not so much in what one does as in the mental attitudes toward it. It's easiest to see this if we take extreme examples. Our television sets and highways are crowded on weekends with people who are not looking for leisure but are running away from it. Leisure goes to a hockey game to see a game: distraction or boredom goes to see one team trample the other into the ice. Leisure drives a car to see the country: boredom drives it to get in front of the car ahead. Leisure is not afraid of solitude, quiet, or unplanned stretches of time; boredom has to have noise, crowds, and constant panic. Leisure goes to a movie to see a play; boredom goes to get enough of a sexy or violent or sentimental shock to forget about real life for a while. Leisure doesn't feel put upon when asked to

take some civic responsibilities; boredom never contributes anything to society: it can't think or create or help others; all it can do is try to forget that job that comes back on Monday morning. (Frye 2002: 224)

We should all pick leisure. Frye is clearly of the view that our approach to culture is characterized by an ethical dimension. Of course, we need to take on board the fact that he presents this as an exaggerated account of a cleavage in our response. But he clearly feels that the less-exaggerated version amounts to an organic division in mental attitude, and it leads us towards a conclusion about culture and mental attitude: the attitude which accepts discipline and application is far better than the attitude which sees little or no value in such application.

This new context helps us to understand common culture. Common culture involves egalitarian national culture, but it also involves a particular mental attitude. The cultural life of our first hypothetical consumer of culture is a match for common culture thus far defined. The cultural life of the second, no matter how national it is, is not. The former is the common-culture ideal.

IV

We have addressed the two main points raised in chapter 1 (addressing the second point in two separate sections). We now have a better idea of what common culture is. In the United Kingdom, to revert to our default, it is enjoying national parks and following professional sports events; it's enjoying the popular music of places like Liverpool, Manchester and Glasgow; it's enjoying the middle-strata visual arts of Glasgow, St Ives and London; it is enjoyment of the literature of London, Leeds, Glasgow, Belfast and many more places. It's taking pleasure in the cityscapes of British cities. It's enjoying the middle-strata work of British composers from different ages and different localities.

Knowledge of domestic common culture helps produce cultural equality. It also results in awareness of the identities of the numerous areas of one's country. In connection with the second point, as we gain knowledge of the variety of the culture-scape and its identities, something else begins to emerge. The more common culture we know, the more we can make out the larger identity that is slowly getting thrown into relief through our awareness of different identities. Of course, that identity is not the whole of national identity: because two strata have been excluded, the identity is not fully defined. But that identity is perceptible, and, what is more important, while everyone's culture is a little different from everyone else's, and while one group supplements its common culture with high culture and the other supplements it with the disfavoured popular, everyone can make out the same larger identity.

It may be useful to bring this set of considerations to a conclusion by turning to the issue of variations on common culture, with reference to UK common culture. The development of common culture would remove differences in the cultural lives of distinct social groups. This will, of course, be a positive development because such differences speak to hierarchies involving the said groups, as we have seen. To give an example of a distinction of this type which might be eliminated by the development of common culture, in *Social Class in the 21st Century*, the authors also reveal how cultural lives are also divided along age lines in the UK: the younger and the older demographics exhibit significantly different patterns of taste and participation. But if a common culture (as I have defined it) were to emerge in the United Kingdom, some of these differences would simply disappear. This becomes clear enough if we turn to music. The younger demographic likes rap, and feels indifferent to classical, heavy metal and jazz; in addition to going to opera, ballet and classical music concerts, the older cohort dislikes pop, reggae, rap and rock – it admits to liking only classical (2015: 111). But as a common culture emerged, such distinctions between older and younger would partly disappear – common culture shepherds us away from our differences.

Might common culture lead to an unappealing conformity of taste, one might ask? In his seminal consideration of common culture, 'The Idea of Common Culture', Raymond Williams raises the question of whether common culture would inevitably amount to a 'uniform and conformist culture' ([1967] 2014: 100).

There are grounds for optimism. In the Introduction I signalled that there are aspects of the elementary level of culture which are obviously extraneous to common culture. That area covers how we dress, our various cuisines, and so on. More importantly, it may well be that, paradoxically, common culture leaves enough room for full cultural individuality. The two middle levels of a national culture offer an embarrassment of riches; at any rate, enough for a personal variation for practically everyone. Such individual taste is compatible with common culture because an individual taste may still qualify as common.

That said, it may be wise to assume that, given the prominence of identity concerns today and the ability on the part of researchers to find commonalities in groups, what we may find is that common culture takes many *different* forms corresponding to the kinds of identities that are also important to people today: identities tied in with gender, race and ethnicity, religion, nationality, etc.

An example will hopefully clarify what an identity-shaped common-culture variation would look like. Let's return to our rugby-watching Dickens enthusiast, whom I mentioned a moment ago. Suppose I have only told half his story. Let's say our hypothetical consumer of common culture is actually Scottish. The British common culture he enjoys includes a *stronger* admixture of Scottish culture than the common culture of some of his Welsh and English neighbours. In other words, his Scottish identity is important to him, even though he does not think of Scottish culture as the whole of his national culture. In addition to his love of Dickens and C.S. Lewis and a plethora of other children's authors, he greatly enjoys different types of Scottish literature as well, all material characteristic of the two middle levels. In addition to the writers of islands and the north of the country, he enjoys the works of James Kelman, Alasdair Gray, Liz Lochhead, and other writers who came to prominence in the 1990s. The nineteenth century is probably his favourite period of Scottish literature. He sees it as a Golden Age of children's literature: it is the age of Stevenson, Barry and George McDonald. But his taste extends to Scottish Gothic; perhaps his favourite novel is James Hogg's great classic *The Private Memoirs and Confessions of a Justified Sinner*. He has even dabbled in earlier Scottish literature: the works of the Jacobean Castalian Band. He is also a Gaelic speaker, and he has read and reread the poetry of Sorley MacLean ever since he was a boy. He also watches a fair amount of BBC Scotland television programmes and listens to BBC Radio Scotland. Some of the music he does listen to is Scottish popular music. In sum, his common culture is a common-culture variant.

But how do we make sure that variations don't result in hierarchies? Common culture can only collapse under the pressure of too much divergence. Would such a variation speak to a subordinate identity? I think it is questions of this type which further theoretical considerations of common culture might address. Essentially, when do variations of common culture speak to dominant and subordinate identities? To what extent can we avoid conformity while enjoying common culture? These are different iterations of the same question, and future theory of common culture might profitably look for answers to that question.

3. Objections and Responses

On National Cultures

In the previous chapter, we gave consideration to the idea that, owing to the itinerant identities of so many of the artists of the modern age, we should categorize their work under the heading of a kind of super-category: the transnational artist. I expressed scepticism about this super-category, suggesting that it might not be the optimal way of providing context for the artists of every age and also that multiple national contexts might be a better way of locating artists associated with more than one place. But what of the works themselves? Might it not be better if we avoid the national context and discuss literature and the other arts within a global context? In our day, it is fashionable when working with culture to shift to the global, and turn our focus to world culture. Recent studies of culture move from the national to the global, with studies of 'world literature' blazing a trail for other disciplines. While not every study coming out of this field encourages a post-national perspective, in many instances such work dismisses the idea of separable national cultures.

One world literature scholar, for example, speaks of the notion that when working with culture, the global or planetary is the only worthwhile context.[1] 'What is the appropriate scale for the study of culture and, in particular, the study of literature?' asks Dimock at the start of her 'Planetary Time and Global Transition: "Context" in Literary Studies'.

My own conclusion is that literary studies requires the largest possible scale, that its appropriate context or unit of analysis is nothing less than the full length and width of our human history and habitat. I make this claim from the standpoint of literature as a linguistic form with agency in the world, a linguistic form compelling action. This action gives rise to a jurisdictional order whose boundaries, while not always supranational, are nonetheless not dictated in advance by the chronology and territory of the nation-state. As a set of temporal and spatial coordinates, the nation is not only too brief, too narrow, but also too predictable in its behavior, its sovereignty uppermost, its borders defended with force if necessary. It is a prefabricated box. Any literature crammed into it is bound to appear more standardized than it is: smaller, tamer, duller, conforming rather than surprising. The randomness of literary action — its unexpected readership, unexpected web of allegiance — can be traced only when that box is momentarily suspended, only when the nation-state is recognized as a necessary but insufficient analytic domain, ceding its primacy upon scale enlargement. (2003: 489)

In the second half of her article, Dimock performs the kind of critical operation she advocates in the first part. When we encounter the exact kind of procedure advocated by the author, it becomes clear that it is a matter of tracing the path of a kind of 'spirit' which passes from one writer to another, as they converse with one another across centuries and continents. Thoreau accessed the spirit of the *Bhagavad Gita*, and (we learn) wrestled with it, producing his own attitudes to non-violence; in the US that attitude to violence was imbibed by Martin Luther King Jr.; and Gandhi, who read English translations of the sacred text, was deeply influenced by Thoreau's attitude to disobedience and non-violence.

The import of her argument is that a focus on anything other than world culture/literature incapacitates the cultural critic. A brave new world of commentary committed to culture and 'planetary time' might yield a new kind of knowledge of global culture. The story of national cultures was always a canard, and volumes about national cultures – volumes about Italian painting, English literature, etc. – always have an in-built limitation.

Is there a significant challenge to the idea of working with national cultures in her argument? I would suggest that we must answer in the negative. Misconceptions abound in such dismissals of national culture. Let's consider three such misconceptions. First, proponents of this theoretical approach argue that literature is not limited by time and space, that the work of an author may impact on that of another who may belong to an entirely different culture, and that the resulting creations testify to extra-national influences. It remains true, however, that an enormous amount of influence has been domestic. In Bloom's famous *Anxiety of Influence*, the author provides abundant detail about the ebb and flow of influence across nations and within the larger English-speaking world, but also, to an enormous extent, within the UK itself.

Second, a focus on the national has never signalled an exclusion of foreign literature and art. Studies of one artist will inevitably discuss the impact of a foreign artist or movement, which means that such knowledge is characterized by *connecting tissue* as well. Of course, comparative studies provide us with a great deal of important connecting knowledge, and the field benefits from the connections afforded by the comparative turn. But single-culture studies furnish us with connections too. From where I am sitting, I can see on one of my bookshelves Benjamin Earle Washburn's study of the impact of *A Thousand and One Nights* on English literature.[2] Scholarship about Henry Fielding references Cervantes; studies of English Romanticism allude to Rousseau; a discussion of Blake includes knowledge of Swedenborg, and so on.[2]

Third, the larger wholes – perhaps even global culture –

are not ruled out by the focus on the national either. There is no antithesis between knowledge production which is quite focused on national cultures, on the one hand, and larger knowledge categories, on the other. That comes down to how we *organize* knowledge. We may organize knowledge in particular ways so that different kinds of supranational units emerge: European literary Romanticism, Baroque music, etc.; perhaps even world literature. If we take, for example, the study of Arthurian literature, such literature is pan-European, and a large number of European countries have produced scholarship about it. When we bring the expertise of different scholars together, a fascinating European vision of the Arthurian emerges, even if scholars often work with national varieties of the literary phenomenon. To return one last time to my bookshelf, next to the volumes already mentioned, I see *The History of Arthurian Scholarship* (edited by Norris J. Lacy), which gathers together essays dealing with French, German, English, Dutch, Scandinavian, etc. Arthurian-literature studies.

The most significant critique of Dimock's thesis, however, must be that, whatever the contours of the story of influence are, none of her discussion proves that national cultures are unviable 'units of analysis'. Indeed, one can expand 'context' without losing sight of national literatures. Ultimately, after all, we should move beyond the notion of 'influence' to something along the lines of 'meaningful and relevant context' when studying literature, with no fear of losing sight of the level of the national. Frye concludes that the proper context for the study of literature is nothing less than the whole of literature:

Every poem must be examined as a unity, but no poem is an isolatable unity. Every poem is inherently connected with other poems of its kind, whether explicitly, as *Lycidas* is with Theocritus and Virgil, or implicitly, as Whitman is with the same tradition, or by anticipation, as *Lycidas* is with later pastoral elegies. And, of course, the kinds or genres of literature are not separable either, like the orders of pre-Darwinian biology. Everyone who has seriously studied literature knows that he is not simply moving from poem to poem, or from one aesthetic experience to another: he is also entering into a coherent and progressive discipline. For literature is not simply an aggregate of books and poems and plays: it is an order of words. And our total literary experience, at any given time, is not a discrete series of memories or impressions of what we have read, but an imaginatively coherent body of experience.

It is literature as an order of words, therefore, which forms the primary context of any given work of literary art. (2005: 32)

But, of course, such a perspective in no way contradicts the option of studying national literature. Indeed, Frye did much to advance the understanding of Canadian literature.

There would seem to be a fear of the parochial in work which inveighs against national culture. In this context, there is no need to be haunted by that spectre, however. The point that we need to engage with culture beyond our national boundaries was highlighted in the Introduction, and important reasons were provided at that stage. Other significant factors heave into view at this point, and this is an opportune moment to give them a little consideration.

I commented in the Introduction that one reason why culture beyond our national borders is essential is tied in with the need to avoid parochialism. We can also advance a defence of domestic culture in relation to how it enhances our experience of foreign cultures – our knowledge of national culture actually helps us to engage meaningfully with other cultures. As usual, it is instructive to use as a guide Hoggart, who, in one of his

Reith lectures, speaks powerfully about the need for balance with respect to national culture and other cultures, and how our understanding of cultures other than our own is enhanced by our appreciation of our own culture:

> No culture has the whole truth or a truth so particular that it will be irreparably violated by contact with others. We can connect, we have to connect: not by hands-across-the-sea junketings or by the solemnities of most attempts at "international understanding", but by a fully faced realisation of common qualities, the ribs of the universal human grammar. If we are to respond anything like fully to cultures not our own it helps to have known, known sensitively and intelligently, our own culture. Our own culture will be a prison unless we can surmount it and become in a certain sense cultureless, international. Yet internationalism is a shallow grave unless we know something about what roots are, and how strongly they affect us all our lives. (Hoggart 1972: 13)

Nor is there any contradiction between an emphasis on the national and our breaking through the boundaries of Eurocentrism. In the present context, the import of this option is that common culture may be easily combined with a particular version of multiculturalism, namely Anthony Kronman's. In Kronman's account, a second version of multiculturalism simply amounts to supplementing our experience of Western culture with non-Western culture. His description of that moderate version is worth quoting at length:

> The benign conception starts from the proposition that in today's world, where a variety of economic, technological and political factors are drawing the peoples of the planet into ever closer contact (a phenomenon usually

described as "globalization"), some understanding and appreciation of non-Western cultures is imperative for any young person who hopes to be able to act in this world in an intelligent and responsible fashion. For Westerners, appreciation of this sort was once a luxury – the province of specialists and connoisseurs. Today, it is a necessity. We are all, increasingly, citizens of the planet, confronted with questions and burdened with responsibilities that go far beyond our membership in this or that national community and our accidental, natal allegiance to a particular culture or tradition. Many who hold this view maintain that the education of every undergraduate in America today ideally ought to include a serious and sustained exposure to the art, literature, and historical experience of one or more of the world's non-Western civilizations – of China, for example, or India or Japan or Islam, or the civilization of South and Central America. Every thoughtful college and university teacher will see the good sense in this proposal, which represents a necessary step toward enlightened and responsible membership in the ecumenical community we now inhabit. (2007: 165-166)

To focus on British literature, while we are studying that national literature – whether it's British Francophone material, British Latin works (in translation, no doubt), Celtic literature or British Anglophone material, which might just as easily be Middle English rather than Modern English material – we may also be studying the literature of Greece and Rome, classics of Indian and Chinese literature, as well as modern French, Italian and German literature, for example. And no doubt the more we know our own national literature, the deeper the appreciation of those other literatures will be.

II

On Judgements About the Popular

As already mentioned, a great many of today's cultural Marxist thinkers have invested in the notion that value judgements about levels of culture are coded judgements about the people who enjoy the culture in question. In the chapter before this one, the discussion moved beyond value judgements to consider which strata of culture qualify as common culture – I spoke of the suitability of strata. But, of course, that stage of the argument does rely on the earlier use of a value judgement to separate the favoured from the disfavoured popular, and so a value judgement is a kind of lynchpin in the argumentation. Hence, my argument runs contrary to the critique of cultural Marxists. Let's turn to one particular iteration of that critique and consider its import.

Mick Hume has argued compellingly against value judgements in our dealings with culture. Hume is a commentator who has a background in Marxism but has warmed to the ethos of liberalism (or even libertarianism) as well as populism, although his populism is aimed at tipping the scales away from elites. The above conclusion about coded judgements characterizes the thinking of Hume. Disgust for tabloids, for example, should be understood as a thinly-veiled expression of contempt for the people who read them. 'The disdain expressed towards tabloid or popular newspapers and the "mass media"', argues Mick Hume, 'is at root a reflection of the contempt felt for the people who consume and sometimes enjoy them' (2012: 59). Here the challenge is aimed specifically at normative thinking about the superiority of what I am calling the favoured over the disfavoured popular, so the critique is decidedly apposite. 'What exactly is wrong with giving the public what they want?' this kind of commentator asks. This viewpoint fleshes out the fact that the attitude I am defending is premised upon a desire to *help* the low-status, to shepherd them towards the 'right' kind of culture. The political problems with this, it is true, can seem axiomatic. It comes off as hopelessly *patrician*.

Hume's challenge is important, but there are ways of countering it. The framework I have introduced here generates some wiggle room when it comes to judgements about cultural value. We make negative value judgements about cultural consumption limited to popular but poorly-executed material when we adopt this way of understanding. But here the context for the judgement is a very particular one. Here such a judgement is an integral part of a concern regarding a common culture, which is *egalitarian* in its attitude.

Also rendering the negative judgement of disfavoured popular culture less unpalatable is the fact that this framework ultimately demotes (in this particular context) the importance of the material at the top end of the schema – it is outside common culture, etc. It is clearly a framework that highlights the downside of a taste for nothing but upper category material – although we have already conceded that that taste is fast becoming a thing of the past as omnivore taste emerges.

We might profitably revisit the critique of cultural populism at this point as well. The theory of the two lower levels of culture is in better shape than the theory of the other levels on account of Hoggart's work, and he helps us to counter the contentions of commentators like Hume. Let's return to Hoggart's thoughts on the popular, picking up from where we left off in chapter 1.

In our day, Jan-Werner Müller has argued that political populism relies on an illusion. It's impossible to 'know the people': 'the whole people never can be grasped or represented' (2017: 28), he comments. The same scepticism characterizes Hoggart's thoughts on cultural populism. The problem with the idea that people know what they want, says Hoggart, is that it is usually the case that an arbiter makes different kinds of culture available to people. Hence the public is always choosing what it wants from a particular range of offerings. And when we factor in that middleman, the idea of people picking what they want becomes somewhat illusory. Speaking of the 'persuading media', Hoggart offers a characterization of the kind of figure who has internalized the ethos of commercialism:

People of that kind, particularly, make use of one of the defender's favourite rejoinders: that they truly reflect the character of their audiences, or they would not succeed. "We speak to and for the Common Man; we are his voice", as one editor of a popular newspaper put it. There is some truth in that. If the world they present were alien to their audiences, they would soon be without audiences. They must speak to some attitudes, some hopes and fears, some prejudices, some enthusiasms and some limitations. But only some at any given time, and others at no time; there must be selection. There is, to take an extreme example, little or no room in this world for any intellectual or imaginative interests – for, say, poets – except in the occasional advert which produces a stereotype and makes fun of it...These operators almost entirely ignore the arts; their "mind-set", or that projected on to their audience is thoroughly low-level, and confident in being so...

They ignore whole ranges of, let us say, working class life or present it only in caricature; as with neighbourliness or, at the other extreme, narrow xenophobia. So they miss much (and though much remains) in general they know what buttons they need to press, buttons which are true to some common attitudes, not the whole truth but enough to allow the claim that these voices do not speak for, reflect, "ordinary folk". "Giving the people what the people want" is not a simple process; it requires an ear and eye able to detect those attitudes which are true to people, but not the whole truth, and which serve the needs of the writer or the writer's employer's purposes. (2004: 45-46)

Additionally, and on a more general level, Hoggart puts a different spin on value judgements about 'low culture'. As we have seen, such judgements can be construed as an attack on the people with a taste for such culture, but, suggests Hoggart, the refusal to make such judgements might just as easily be construed as a wrongheaded attitude encouraging the less well-off to adopt a non-aspirational attitude to culture. In a highly appealing turn of phrase, a contemporary rhetorician has warned against the 'soft bigotry of low expectations'. Hoggart foreshadows this sentiment when, with reference to Aneurin Bevan, he speaks of 'the poverty of expectations' (2004: 17). The idea that there is no need for mobility in the cultural domain, tied in with denying that some work is more valuable than others, is anathema to Hoggart. In effect, it is as if we say to people 'stay as sweet as you are':

> To anyone from a bookless home the suggestion that there should be such an approach to literature, a prior social filtering rather than a judgement of different qualities, is offensive and ill-judged. The thought that such a creed is being offered up to people who still live in a bookless culture, as a justification for being satisfied with the popular press, the shoddier television programmes and other such barbarisms, is yet another instance of the "stay as sweet as you are" syndrome. (1996: 59)

III

Of course, Frye's conclusions about leisure and boredom also fly in the face of those of Bourdieuians who encourage us to think of distinctions in a highly political manner. The paradigm that these scholars work with insists on 'reading' distinctions such as this one as part of the problem: a distinction between boredom and leisure is exactly the kind of thought which buttresses inequalities in society.

Much of what was said in chapter 1 is obviously germane here, and the reader may profitably bring to mind what has already been said. If all value judgements attached to the two attitudes were to be avoided, would an *entente* really prevail? In the Introduction, we saw how Hoggart warns us that 'tolerance' is merely a halfway house to compulsory cultural populism, and the same could apply here: the critique of the implied value judgement might easily result in inverted snobbery and seriousness of attitude towards culture becoming socially disfavoured. Additionally, an accepting attitude towards what Frye classes as 'boredom' might easily be construed, once more, as cultural populism and an example of the 'stay as sweet as you are' syndrome. Moreover, we should also say in Frye's defence that his position on inequality is clear enough. The classless society stands as the ideal in his work. 'Antidemocratic activity', he argues, 'consists in trying to put class distinctions on some permanent basis' (2003a: 255). He advocates an economic situation in which people in society can rely on, first, equality of opportunity and, subsequently, full equality (see Graham 2011: 77-98).

We might, however, at this point provide an additional response to the challenge represented by the Bourdieu-type critique of value judgements. For at this stage, another 'defence' offers itself as well. And that defence, quite fortuitously, reveals more of the political backdrop to the present study.

Frye on Arnold and the Classless Society

Let's proceed by considering the larger political context of what has been said thus far. Rehearsing the view of the 'bourgeois liberal' (2000a: 172), Frye states that liberalism is:

the doctrine that society cannot attain freedom except by individualizing its culture. It is only when the individual is enabled to form an individual synthesis of ideas, beliefs, and tastes that a principle of freedom is established in society. (2003a: 257)

Frye has no interest in underestimating the significance of the aspects of civil society which sustain individual liberty, but the means are secondary to the ends. Speaking of the loyalty we might feel for democracy, he argues that democracy 'does not mean only the machinery of elections, or a greater tolerance of religion or art or a greater relaxation of leisure, privacy or freedom of movement, but what all these things point to: the sense of individuality that grows out of society but is infinitely more than a social function' (2006: 119).

It might appear that Frye's understanding is close to an idea of the individual that is connected to today's identity politics and the legacy of Rousseau. Fukuyama argues that a rogue liberal tradition spearheaded by Rousseau bequeathed to us the notion that everyone has a unique inner self (2019: 53-54) – which in turn produced the twentieth-century self-esteem cult, the consequent therapeutic approach to life, and, ultimately, identity politics.[3] But the differences are clear enough when we consider the idea of self advanced by identity politics. Focusing on the self and education, Mark Lilla suggests that the humanities and social sciences of today are primarily focused upon identity. The student, he argues, 'is likely to draw the conclusion that the aim of education is not to progressively become a self through engagement with the wider world. Rather, one engages with the world and particularly politics for the limited aim of understanding and affirming what one already is' (2017: 84). Such an approach, argues Lilla, means that much of what the student traditionally studied now belongs to hinterlands of irrelevance. Continuing his sketch of the typical student's education and identity, he adds that

> Her political interest will be real but circumscribed by the confines of her self-definition. Issues that penetrate those confines now take on looming importance and her position on them quickly becomes non-negotiable; those issues that don't touch her identity are not even perceived. (2017: 85)

The difference between this account of individuality and Frye's should be clear enough.

Liberalism draws on the legacy of thinkers ranging from Grotius, Hobbes and Locke, to Montesquieu, Constant and Tocqueville, among others. Frye's liberalism is grounded in the writings of John Milton, Matthew Arnold and J. S. Mill. In Frye's view, Arnold's view of freedom represents a secularized version of Milton's religious understanding of liberty.[4] For Frye, as for Matthew Arnold, individuality does not emerge through the simple business of doing whatever one likes; doing as one likes is anarchism of the ego rather than liberty. Individual freedom is largely a question of developing skills through sustained effort:

> Genuine freedom and discipline are the same thing: one cannot be set free to play the piano or speak German without a long period of directed attention and practice. But for most people freedom means only what Arnold called doing as one likes, that is, getting pushed around by one's inner impulses. (2000b: 491)

Mill's contribution is to emphasize the notion that the development of individuality should be allowed to emerge without encumbrance. These different views of liberalism are interwoven in the simple observation that we must be free to develop our individuality. Frye turns to the kind of society suggested by such a liberalism in *The Double Vision*. Contrasting 'primitive' and 'mature' societies, he provides us with a tableau of a society of individuality which, he states, is the goal of the bourgeois liberal attitude. His account is suggestive of the influence of Arnold and Mill as well as Milton:

> A primitive or embryonic society is one in which the individual is primarily thought of as a function of the social group...A mature society, in contrast, understands that its primary aim is to develop a genuine individuality in its members. In a fully mature society the structure of authority becomes a function of the individuals within it, all of them, without distinctions of sex, class, or race, living, loving, thinking, and producing with a sense of space around them. (2000a: 171)

But Frye's thinking is organized around *three* values and corresponding societal sectors. We might proceed by contrasting the political and economic sectors, government and industry. 'The modern world', Frye suggests, 'began with the Industrial Revolution and the Industrial Revolution set up an economic structure beside the political one which was really a rival form of society' (2003a: 48). In Frye's account, these societies are connected to contrasting values: equality (industry) and liberty (politics), the first value considered. In one revealing statement, he provides a potted history of how successful battles were fought for those values:

> The evolution of political democracy, as it fought against entrenched privilege at first, and then against dictatorial tendencies, has to some extent been a genuine evolution of an idea of liberty, however often betrayed and perverted, and however much threatened still. The evolution of industry into a society of producers, as labour continued to fight against

a managerial oligarchy, has been to a correspondingly modified extent an evolution of an idea of equality. (2003a: 57)

Also of great interest to Frye is the leisure sector. Up to a point, leisure represents a discrete sector: it is easily distinguishable from government and the economy. And, as we shall see presently, it is associated with a third value. But in terms of the activity associated with leisure there is a significant overlap between leisure and liberty. For, ultimately, it is leisure activities, associated with the leisure sector, which foster liberty in society. The difference between the domains of liberty and leisure becomes clearer when we turn to the value associated with leisure, which is the third revolutionary value: fraternity. Fraternity is what emerges in relation to the *sharedness* of liberty or individuality. Frye's point is that individuality does not exist in a social vacuum, and a mature society is not simply an aggregate of individuals; individuality also results in common ground between individuals. 'A society of students, scholars, and artists', he asserts, 'is a society of neighbours' (2003a: 58). (Frye is at pains to give this neighbourliness an international character, but it is also applicable to national fraternity.[5]) Here we can catch a glimpse of how Frye would think of cultural inequality. It is the situation in which separate fraternities make up a hierarchy. Liberty and fraternity are also connected through their association with education. Frye has a pronounced interest in foregrounding the extent to which a person's intellectual life – their 'synthesis of ideas, beliefs, and tastes' – is identifiable with education. As we have already seen, when the focus is liberty in Frye's writings, the stress falls on practice and the development of skills rather than simple fun, and this makes possible the identification of the intellectual life with education. At the outset, we learned that these associations or identifications carry over into his discussions of leisure:

'education is the positive aspect of leisure', he observes on another occasion (2003a: 49). Consequently, Frye is prepared to speak figuratively of our *group* engagement with culture, along with science and philosophy, as a university without walls. In effect, he extends Arnold and Mill's thinking about liberty into education, which is the site of something fraternal:

> it might be well to recast our conception of the [university] along the wider lines indicated by Arnold's conception of culture or Mill's conception of an area of free discussion... Wherever two or three are discussing a subject in complete freedom, with regard only to the truth of the argument; wherever a group is united by a common interest in music or drama or the study of rocks or plants; wherever conversation moves from news and gossip to serious issues and principles, there the University, in the wider sense, is at work in society. (2000b: 62).[6]

By this stage, it is clearly a somewhat expanded idea of 'leisure' which seems to structure Frye's thinking; but everything Frye says about that larger concept of leisure applies equally to the one we have been working with until now, which remains our main interest.

Frye's outlook seems to speak to an ideal combination of liberty, equality and fraternity, suggestive of a combination of conservative, radical and liberal sympathies. In this respect, Frye's reading of Matthew Arnold is apposite. As Frye explains, in Arnold's view, when it comes to how we organize society, there is no sense in allowing any of the three social classes or their ideologies to rise to the fore. Arnold is, of course, sardonic in his treatment of the classes, employing a parodic terminology for them: the aristocracy is renamed the barbarians, the middle class the Philistines, and the working class the populace. In connection with each class, he speaks of the ordinary self –

that aspect of oneself which matches one's class. It is only the ordinary self, in each case, Arnold argues, that seeks to rule over others. Thus, neither the rule of the leisure class, nor the liberalism of the middle class, nor the Jacobinism of the working class will do. Class values get embodied in classes (each of which is power-hungry), Frye explains, and

> their jockeying for power hinders and retards the growth of culture: it would have seemed the wildest paradox to Arnold to think of arriving at a classless society through increasing the ascendancy of one of its classes. Reactivating the aristocracy, as Carlyle was urging, would merely create a new barbarism; the dictatorship of the proletariat would reduce society to a "populace", and the ascendancy of the bourgeoisie in Arnold's own Victorian England was producing only Philistinism. (2009a: 114)[7]

Even more importantly, a society of all three values would be a classless society. Crucially, the all-important political values are the values of the three social classes, a factor which, given how each political value is vaunted by Arnold and Frye, suggests the combination of conservative, radical and liberal sympathies. Though liberty in Western societies extends to the working class, Arnold associates such freedom with the middle class: 'liberty is the specifically middle-class contribution to the classless society of genuine culture' (2005: 320). Similarly, equality has a class connection: it is the specifically working-class contribution to the same society (ibid.). Completing the picture, Frye associates fraternity with a social class, specifically the aristocracy, the old leisure class, as it were. The connection is derived from Arnold: it is implicit if not explicit in Arnold's work, Frye suggests (2009a: 115). (When speaking of culture, Arnold is emphatic about the importance of 'the best which has been thought and said', which might make us think of the 'aristocracy', etymologically, the rule by the best.) Against such a backdrop, it is easy to identify 'the three classes of society, upper, middle, and lower, as elements in the ultimate classless society towards which "culture" leads' (2009a: 114).

On Attitude to Leisure

To return to our main concern, it is Frye's preferred mental attitude to culture – the one characterized by seriousness and responsibility – that might represent an indispensable feature of the classless society he describes. Leisure as distraction appears to belong to another society all together. This point gets thrown into sharp relief when we turn to a discussion in Frye's work where he strategically reduces his three-sector model to two, thereby fleshing out the importance of a serious-minded engagement with culture. He begins by sketching an outline of a nineteenth-century understanding of leisure and work, where the two activities are strongly associated with two social classes. When the two activities belong to separate classes, free-time activities are relief from work or the decadent amusement of the ruling class:

> As long as we think of society, in nineteenth-century terms, as essentially productive, leisure is only spare time, usually filled up with various forms of distraction, and a "leisure class", which has nothing but spare time, is only a class of parasites. (2003a: 49)

If it is typical of such a set-up that leisure amounts to distraction, it becomes an atavistic understanding when, in a better societal setting, leisure and work become activities of the same class and the same lives:

> But as soon as we realize that leisure is as genuine and important an aspect of everyone's life as remunerative work,

leisure becomes something that also demands discipline and responsibility. Distraction, of the kind one sees on highways and beaches at holiday weekends, is not leisure but a running away from leisure, a refusal to face the test of one's inner resources that spare time poses. (2003a: 49-50)

As we move into a better society, our understanding of leisure gets transformed. In this new situation, to view leisure as distraction is characteristic of an earlier phase of societal development; it is an outdated option.

If we go back to our two consumers of culture, introduced in the third section of chapter 2, it is clear that the second consumer might profitably adopt an attitude to culture closer to his friend's. The framework I have outlined clarifies that the situation in which the two attitudes persist amounts to one in which one societal group enjoys culture in a manner which suggests the realities of the unity of work and leisure, while another group lives a cultural life which suggests denial of those new realities.

It could be objected that Frye's writings on leisure are part of a culture of how we think about leisure which came to the fore in the 1960s before losing credibility as an analysis of where society was headed. Reading the following passage today, we are struck by its bright-eyed optimism:

Today, the machinery of production appears to be steadily declining in the proportion of time and attention that it requires. I am not speaking of automation, which is not a cause but an effect of this process: I mean simply that the proportion of work to leisure which according to the Book of Genesis was established by God himself on a ratio of six to one is rapidly changing in the direction a ratio of one to one...We appear, then, to be entering a period in which work and leisure are not embodied in different classes, but should be thought of as two aspects, nearly equal in importance, of the same life. Every citizen may not be only a Martha, troubled about many things, but a Mary who has chosen the better part [Luke 10:38–42], and the question, "What does he know?" becomes as relevant to defining one's social function as the question, "What does he do?" (2000b: 271)

Published in 1966, a piece like this is clearly a part of the writing culture of 'the society of abundance', which many writers of the time hoped for. But that society never materialized. 'Ten or 20 years later', comments Howard Brick, speaking of confident predictions of an age of plenty, 'the claim appeared to some observers a mark of the complacency, excessive optimism, or even the utopian folly of the 1960s' (Brick 2000: 1).

Of course, as indicated at the outset, this study is written in a utopian idiom; it is not about what is likely but about what is possible and desirable. It advocates, in one regard, cultural equality but also the improved economic circumstances necessary for that equality. In other words, in as much as there is insufficient leisure time combined with work, this study advocates more leisure, as well as the abundance which permits its burgeoning.

Part III

4. Common-Culture British Literature

In this chapter and the two chapters after it, the focus returns to the UK context. I have evolved a two-tier understanding of common culture on an abstract and general level. The next thing to do is take a close look at the exact nature of UK common-culture material in specific domains. We begin with British common-culture literature.[1] Much of what follows will be relevant in relation to considerations of other countries' common-culture literature, even if my focus is the UK.

Discernible in the literary theory of Northrop Frye is a four-level understanding of British literature, and therefore an account of what might constitute British common-culture literature. Of course, Frye does not focus exclusively on British literature. At times he speaks in the most general terms of literature; mostly, his focus is Anglophone literature. But it is easy to derive a rough picture of British common-culture literature from his work, even if that picture will be almost exclusively about Anglophone works. British literature is the epicentre of his writing about Anglophone literature, after all. In what follows, I will emphasize his references to British literature, so that a clear vision of British common-culture literature is allowed to emerge.

Frye on Myth and Metaphor

Frye's point of departure is that the basic unit of literature is the archetype. Speaking of the archetypal phase of meaning, he states:

> The symbol in this phase is the communicable unit, to which I give the name archetype: that is, a typical or recurring

image. I mean by an archetype a symbol which connects one poem with another and thereby helps to unify and integrate our literary experience. (2006a: 91-92)[2]

In connection with this starting point, Frye states that the reader of literature should not simply try to understand the particular work he or she has just read. Rather, we need to work on the meaning of literature as a whole, so a single reader should be forever trying to work out the significance of everything he or she has read. In his theoretical work, Frye provides us with an account of the kind of structures which should start to emerge in the mind of the reader as s/he builds up that picture.

Form rather than content is Frye's focus. Form consists of two dimensions, the mythical and the metaphorical. The former is the unit of the latter. When trying to define literary form, critics seek to identify that dimension of literature which is as distant from 'representativeness' as abstract painting or most music is. For Frye, as we move from literary content to literary form, we pass from 'realism', to literary romance, and ultimately to myth. Myth, like music, is pure form, which only takes on 'content' as it moves back to the other pole, which, although a work may impress us as realistic, amounts to a displaced myth.

I'll turn to metaphor in a moment, but, in terms of myth, what should start to emerge as the reader acquires more and more literary knowledge are episodes in a larger mythical narrative. Literature in Frye's view is characterized by astonishing continuity, provided by myth:

Myths of gods merge into legends of heroes; legends of heroes merge into plots of tragedies and comedies; plots of tragedies and comedies merge into plots of more or less realistic fiction. But these are changes of social context rather than of literary form, and the constructive principles of story-telling remain constant through them, though of course, they adapt to them. Tom Jones and Oliver Twist are typical enough as low mimetic characters, but the birth-mystery plots in which they are involved are plausible adaptations of fictional formulas that go back to Menander, and from Menander to Euripides' *Ion*, and from Euripides to legends like those of Perseus and Moses. (2006a: 48)

It is the heroic and mythical structures which are of special interest to us, for the mythical pattern is clearer in such literature. If we turn to Poe's 'Ligeia', for example, considering it in this manner, we become aware of its mythical structure, which can be characterized as the story of Proserpine or what Frye calls, in *Anatomy of Criticism*, the 'mythical death and revival pattern' (2006a: 128).

Importantly, some literary works don't simply exhibit a single mythical pattern: more ambitious works, such as epic poetry, are encyclopaedic in nature, and, consequently, we may detect multiple myths in such works. It is always interesting to turn to Frye's treatment of Blake when discussing myth. Central to Blake's poetic thought is his 'Orc cycle', the story of a revolutionary force which periodically rises and falls. In his discussion of Blake's 'Orc cycle', Frye casts light on the manifold mythical nature of this Blakean myth. A number of mythical patterns are simultaneously present in the narrative:

Orc, then, is not only Blake's Prometheus but his Adonis, the dying and reviving god of his mythology. Orc represents the return of dawn and the spring and all the human analogies of their return: the continuous arrival of new life, the renewed sexual and reproductive power which that brings, and the periodic overthrow of social tyranny. He is both a sun-god, the jocund day on the mountain tops, and a god of renewed "vegetable" or natural human, life. (2004: 208)

Hence, ambitious poetry, like that of Blake's, is a poetry where myths are gathered. It provides us, then, with special access to much of the mythical content of literature.

As regards metaphor, Frye contends that literature is characterized by the 'archetypal metaphor' (Frye 2006a: 115). Speaking of 'archetypal metaphor', he states that 'Archetypally, where the symbol is an associative cluster, the metaphor unites two individual images, each of which is a specific representative of a class or genus' (ibid.), a formulation which needs unpacking. If we start out with classes or geni, Frye often works with categories of Being derived from the idea of the 'Great Chain of Being'.

Class or genus
Divine
Human
Animal
Vegetable
Mineral

Figure 2

Frye refers to an image which is a 'specific representative of its class' (2006a: 115) by which he means that, in this mythical domain, one image of the vegetable world, say the image of a tree, represents the whole genus. In the *Prose Edda* we are told about an ash tree, the 'yggdrasil', which, among other inhabitants, has four stags moving about *in* its branches. Its significance goes beyond this, but, on one level, the tree clearly represents its whole genus – it is a tree which represents all trees, as it were.

If we have understood that it is possible for an image to be a 'specific representative of its class', we can proceed to the other dimension of what Frye says: 'the metaphor unites two individual images, each of which is a specific representative of a class or genus' (ibid.). So, one image of this type gets identified with another image of this type. An obvious model is provided by Christian imagery: the lamb (animal world) is identifiable with the wine and bread of communion (vegetable world symbols). The image of Yggdrasil, just mentioned, provides us with another example: in that image, the same two worlds are apparently being drawn into identification.

The reader might object that there is a whole other dimension to literature; after all, in literature, while some images are pleasant or even paradisal, others are ghastly or even demonic. Clearly, some kind of polarity inheres in literary imagery. The mythical area must be divided into two, which Frye names the apocalyptic and the demonic.

To simplify this somewhat, the apocalyptic column consists of the mythical images which hold great appeal; they relate to the forms which speak to human desire. The demonic column comprises images that are the polar opposite: they inspire fear, dislike or even disgust. His thinking is structured along the lines of the following table (deliberately left empty here):

	Apocalyptic	Demonic
Divine		
Human		
Animal		
Vegetable		
Mineral		

Figure 3

We might profitably return to Frye on Blake at this point.

For Frye, Blake's poetry is full of archetypal metaphor. Indeed, he contends that Blake's poetry consists 'almost entirely in the articulation of archetypes' (2005: 203). To begin with the apocalyptic world, images are specific representatives of their classes in Blake's poetry. In one passage, Frye adroitly takes us through the images of the human, animal, vegetable and minerals categories in Blake's poetry:

> The real form of human society is the body of one man; the flock of sheep is the body of one lamb; the garden is the body of one tree, the so-called tree of life. The city is the body of one building or temple, a house of many mansions, and the building itself is the body of one stone, a glowing and fiery precious stone, the unfallen stone of alchemy which assimilates everything else to itself, Blake's grain of sand which contains the world. (2005:197)

Having identified those images, he goes on to clarify that each is actually a metaphor uniting two individual images representative of a class: the representative of the human level of reality is identical with that of the animal world, that image of the animal world is identifiable with the representative of the vegetable category, and so on:

> The one man is also the one lamb, and the body and blood of the animal form are the bread and wine which are the human forms of the vegetable world. The tree of life is the upright vertebrate form of man; the living stone, the glowing transparent furnace, is the furnace of heart and lungs and bowels in the animal body. The river of life is the blood that circulates within that body. Eden, which according to Blake was a city as well as a garden, had a fourfold river, but no sea, for the river remained inside Paradise, which was the body of one man...

The more developed society is, the more clearly man realizes that a society of gods would have to be, like the society of man, the body of one God. Eventually he realizes that the intelligible forms of man and of whatever is above man on the chain of being must be identical. The identity of God and man is for Blake the whole of Christianity. (2005: 197-8)

The demonic world is characterized by a grotesque mirror image of the apocalyptic world, which means that, even though it is not focused on human desire but on the forms of human fear, it also consists of archetypal metaphor. In his poetry, the demonic world is bound up with what Blake calls 'natural religion': 'natural religion, being a parody of real religion, often develops a set of individuals symbols corresponding to the lamb, the tree of life, the glowing stone, and the rest', Frye explains (2005: 198-199). Hence:

Against the tree of life we have what Blake calls the tree of mystery, the barren fig tree, the dead tree of the cross, Adam's tree of knowledge, with its forbidden fruit corresponding to the fruits of healing on the tree of life. Against the fiery precious stone, the bodily form in which John saw God "like a jasper and a sardine stone", we have the furnace, the prison of heat without light which is the form of the opaque warm-blooded body in the world of frustration, or the stone of Druidical sacrifice like the one that Hardy associates with Tess. Against the animal body of the lamb, we have the figure that Blake calls, after Ezekiel, the Covering Cherub, who represents a great many things, the unreal world of gods, human tyranny and exploitation, and the remoteness of the sky, but whose animal form is that of the serpent or dragon wrapped around the forbidden tree. The dragon, being both monstrous and fictitious, is the best animal representative of the bogies inspired by human inertia: the Book of Revelation calls it "the beast that was, and is not, and yet is". (2005: 199)

Because Blake is such an ambitious poet, we find all these structures in his poetry. But these are the very structures around which the whole of literature is organized. As s/he proceeds, the reader allows these structures to emerge, and details may be added with every work read, so that an ever more complete structure may slowly evolve.

From Popular to Highbrow Literature

This view of literature informs how Frye thinks about the levels of literature, which he divides into four. Let's begin with two kinds of popular literature.

a) Popular Literature

With respect to the first kind of popular literature, which is more a matter of content than form, the *concept* is the principle of popular poetry, and something along the lines of *displaced narrative* is the principle of popular fiction. Labelling the conceptual kind of popular poetry 'vogue poetry', Frye provides us with a small handful of examples:

It talks about the Deity in the eighteenth century, of duty in the nineteenth, or it speaks to the eternal bourgeois in the heart of man, like Kipling's *If*, Longfellow's *Psalm of Life* or Burns's *A Man's A Man for a that*. (2005: 294)

With respect to fiction, Frye's view is that the first kind of popular fiction is characterized by topicality: it may possess 'news value' (2005: 293), as he suggests at one point. But presumably it may be historical as well, its relevance relating to its representation of the past. More generally, he has in mind popular fiction that passes muster as 'realistic', although the safer term is 'displaced'. In Frye's own times, the popular novels of Graham Greene would have provided examples of this kind of material.

There is little connection between Frye's view of myth and metaphor and this first conception of popular literature, but it is central to the second type. He calls it the formally popular, and it is this kind of popular that is of prime importance to us. On a *general* level, Frye is of the view that metaphor is the formal principle of poetry, while myth is the formal principle of fiction, and this distinction determines how he conceptualizes the formally popular. If, in the first context, *the concept* is the principle of popular poetry, and *displaced narrative* is the principle of popular fiction, in the second context, *metaphor* is the principle of popular poetry, and *myth* is the principle of popular fiction.

To begin with poetry, Blake's popular 'The Human Abstract' is an example of the second kind of popular poetry. The tree in his poem is an example of archetypal metaphor: it comprises an identity of the vegetable world and the animal world. The poem offers three images that might be considered representative of the animal world, and the tree is identifiable with each of them: metaphorically, the tree 'is' the raven, as well as the caterpillar and the fly. The poem is yet more metaphorical. The human world also gets identified with the vegetable world: at the end of the poem, the tree is located inside the human body (Blake 1982: 27).

Blake's representative of the vegetable world, a tree of death, belongs, of course, to the demonic structure of imagery. It is the fearful tree that is all fearful trees, if you will. Another popular poem provides us with an *apocalyptic* image that is a representative of the vegetable world, namely Yeats' 'holy tree' from 'The Two Trees'. Yeats's poem, in fact, deals with both trees: the poem is concerned with the contrast between the 'holy tree', on the one hand, and the tree of death also spoken of in the poem, on the other. Interestingly, the metaphor is the same as it is in Blake. The latter tree is identified with 'the ravens of unresting thought', and the former (and probably the latter) also gets identified with the human body – the holy tree, we learn, grows in the beloved's heart.

Turning to fiction, again, Poe's 'Ligeia' of course represents an example of the second kind of popular fiction. As we have seen, it retells the story of Proserpine. Other popular works of this type offer other mythical patterns. *Tom Sawyer*, for example, exhibits a mythical structure. '[If] we "stand back" from *Tom Sawyer*', Frye explains, 'we can see a youth with no father or mother emerging with a maiden from a labyrinthine cave, leaving a bat-eating demon imprisoned behind him' (2006a: 177). Pyle's *The Merry Adventures of Robin Hood* (Pyle 2005) is characterized by a mythical shape, which is best thought of as the myth of the tree-god. When we start thinking about *Lord of the Rings* in this way, we become aware of the renounced quest pattern in the story: Frodo succeeds in his quest when his nerve fails and he starts to give up. In the interactive fiction *Galatea* by Emily Short (Short 2000), it is, of course, the myth of Pygmalion and his creation that provides the author with her inspiration. Lastly, when we turn to Alan Moore's *V for Vendetta* (Moore 1988–89), we become appreciative of the fact that it introduces us to the archetypal story of the killing of the tyrant leader/sacrificed victim (identified by Frye as 'the demonic or undisplaced radical form of tragic or ironic structures' (2006a: 137)). (The myth is actually even clearer in the film adaptation, where 'Adam Sutler' is very obviously a sacrificed victim figure in addition to tyrant leader.)

b) Highbrow Literature
Turning to highbrow literature, such popular characteristics do not simply characterize the formally popular: they characterize much serious Anglophone literature, too, which for Frye means

that, in the case of English literature, there is an enormous affinity between the serious and the popular. But here a distinction can be made. On the one hand, some of the more serious works of English literature are marked by an affinity with the popular, while some others, which may or may not possess popular features, impress us as works which require extended study and significant learning on the part of the readers.

In Frye's view, 'difficult works' are fairly typical of earlier twentieth-century literature, where there is a gap between the serious and the popular (2006a: 46-47), although they are not entirely limited to that period. Such writers' works are mythical, but they are characterized by qualities such as subtly and complexity; such writers are learned and recondite; they require patient study. Not that such learnedness means that the writers in question are less mythical. 'Learned mythopoeia', comments Frye, 'as we have it in the last period of Henry James and in James Joyce, for example, may become bewilderingly complex; but the complexities are designed to reveal and not to disguise the myth' (2006a: 109).

But much of the rest of English literature is characterized by a pronounced connection with the popular. The mode which follows on from modernism is, of course, a type of writing where high and low interpenetrate with one another, as literary criticism has evinced on numerous occasions. For Frye, that new popular mode signifies a *ricorso*, representing 'a return of irony to myth' (2006a: 46), and he undoubtedly thinks of it as a popular mode.

More importantly, much of what we think of as the earlier Anglophone literary heritage is characterized by an affinity with the popular. For Frye, English literature is characterized by three mythopoeic periods: 'one around 1600, the age of Spenser, Shakespeare and the early Milton; one around 1800, the age of Blake and the great Romantics; and one around the period 1920-1950' (2003b: 418). As mentioned, difficulties arise if we try to construe modernist literature as popular, but the period of Blake and the Romantics is also a period when serious literature has a straightforward connection with the popular. In additional to lyrical poetry, this is an age of epic poems, which might impress the reader as unequivocally 'elite' literature. But in Frye's view everything from Blake's *Milton*, to Wordsworth's *Prelude*, Byron's *Don Juan* and Keats' *Hyperion* all show signs of pronounced connections with the popular.[3] At one point in 'Blake After Two Centuries', Frye makes the audacious claim that by 2057, Blake's Prophetic Books will be thought of as works of popular literature:

> At present his prophecies seem to have little to do with popular literature in any sense of the word, but opinion will have changed on this point long before the tercentenary rolls around. It will then be generally understood that just as Blake's lyrics are among the best possible introductions to poetic experience, so his prophecies are among the best possible introductions to the grammar and structure of literary mythology. (2005: 295)

Frye no doubt also has American Romanticism in mind as well when alluding (very loosely) to the age of Blake.

To a significant extent the period around 1600 is also one in which the serious and the popular merge. (Frye clearly has enormous sympathy for Blake's view that the Neoclassical age was an interruption of the main tradition of English literature (2004: 171).) It is true that Milton, for example, can fairly be thought of as an 'elite' writer, but a great many other writers of the period boast popular writer credentials, Shakespeare included.[4] Shakespeare's romances and comedies, for example, are characterized by 'a policy of including some features of a popular, self-contained, highly stylized technique' (2010: 133), although some of his late romances may belong to the category of highbrow and learned.

The Four Levels of Literature

The reader will already have understood that what we have here is a conception of literature which matches my more general and abstract four-level understanding of culture. If we re-introduce the national context and limit our focus to works of British literature, a four-fold organization of British literature emerges:

'Elite'	British Neoclassical literature, literary modernism and other 'difficult writing'
Highbrow and popular (the popular-highbrow)	Serious but popular literary works of the Renaissance, British Romanticism (and post-Romanticism), along with recent romantic and mythical British literature
The favoured popular	Formally popular literary works by British authors (from various ages)
The disfavoured popular	Vogue poetry, bestsellers, etc. from the United Kingdom

Figure 4

The preceding section and the upcoming one provide us with numerous suggestions about the kinds of British literature belonging to the two middle strata and therefore the common culture of the country. On the level of the favoured popular, it is the lyrical poetry of Romantic poets, but also poets of other ages, including the Renaissance and even the twentieth century, as well as prose romances and tales such as those of Gothic writers, Tolkien and British science fiction writers, not to mention other genres such as comedies and ballads and folk songs. On the level of the popular-highbrow, it is more ambitious poetic works, such as epic poems bearing an affinity to the popular, such as Romantic epics, as well as more challenging intellectual satire, tragedy and longer narrative poems.

Cultural Mobility in the Literary Domain

Of course, this raises the question of how those with less literary education may be able to develop an enjoyment of the British literature of the 'highbrow and popular' stratum. Providing an answer takes us well beyond the domain of common-culture material, to which the foregoing observations relate, and into the area of response to culture: specifically, the matter of what literature yields when we approach it with 'discipline and responsibility' (2003a: 49-50).

When theorizing these two kinds of popular literature, Frye distinguishes between literature which is statistically popular, on the one hand, and literature which requires little or no training, on the other. The first kind of popular material is popular in both respects. This second kind of material is tied up with the second characteristic: it may be thought of as popular because it requires little in the way of literary education. Much of it is what we might think of as canonical, but, interestingly, it requires little or no expertise. The formally popular is

> ...the literature that demands the minimum of previous verbal experience and special education from the reader. In poetry, this would include, say, the songs of Burns and Blake, the Lucy lyrics of Wordsworth, ballads and folksongs, and other simple forms ranging from some of the songs and sonnets of Shakespeare to Emily Dickinson. (2006b: 22)

Interestingly, Frye proceeds by stating that such literature should be central to education:

Much if not most of this would be very unpopular in the bestseller sense, but it is the kind of material that should be central in the literary education of children and others of limited contact with words. (2006b: 22)

Of course, here Frye is advocating a particular kind of formal education, one partly centred on the popular. In other statements about the formally popular, however, he drops the reference to formal education. Reading such literature *is* an education. The formally popular is a type of 'escalator culture':

By "popular" we usually mean what is temporarily fashionable, for reasons that can be derived from the social conditions of any given time. But there is a more permanent sense in which a work may be popular, not as a bestseller, but in the sense of providing a key to imaginative experience for the untrained. The popular in this sense is the continuing primitive, the creative design that makes its impact independently of special education. Burns is a popular poet, not in any technical or best-seller sense, but in the sense that he continues and provides modern examples for a primitive tradition of folk song and ballad. (2010: 161)

Frye is of the view that the 'knowledge' of myth and metaphor which the reader acquires through his or her encounter with formally popular literature equips that reader for other, more challenging, highbrow literature. Frye repeats this point time and time again. In 'Blake After Two Centuries', he states that this kind of popular literature represents 'the art which affords a key to imaginative experience for the untrained' (2005: 293). The formally popular, then, has the capacity to eventuate a kind of mobility in literature, whereby readers with less literary experience may quickly acquire a form of training, which allows them to proceed to other kinds of literature. Importantly, such popular literature equips the reader for the literature of the 'highbrow and popular' stratum.

We might profitably rehearse how this can work in practice. Here there is perhaps no need to stick to British literature when considering the training provided by the formally popular: after all, the formally popular of any national literature can furnish us with the training we need for British literature of the 'highbrow and popular' stratum. The story of Tom Sawyer, for example, provides a 'template' for the story in Blake's longer poems of Orc, or for certain episodes it features, at least. A moment ago, we learned that Twain's novel introduces us to a mythical pattern in which 'a youth with no father or mother [emerges] with a maiden from a labyrinthine cave, leaving a bat-eating demon imprisoned behind him' (2006a: 177). The story, then, prefigures episodes of the Orc cycle for the reader. The point becomes clearer if we turn to another account of that cycle in Frye:

> Orc is first shown us, in the *Preludium* to *America*, as the libido of the dream, a boy lusting for a dim maternal figure and bitterly hating an old man who keeps him in chains. Then we see him as the conquering hero of romance, killing dragons and sea monsters, ridding the barren land of its impotent aged kings, freeing imprisoned women, and giving new hope to men. Finally we see him subside into the world of darkness again from whence he emerged, as the world of law slowly recovers its balance. (2004: 200)

The reader derives training from metaphor from the formally popular, too. In one section of Blake's *The Four Zoas*, the action is centred on the 'Tree of Mystery'. The image is actually an archetypal metaphor in which archetypal representatives of the vegetable and animal worlds enter into identification with one another. Urizen, Orc's antagonist, compels Orc to become a serpent and to climb the tree of Mystery:

> ...therefore he made Orc
> In Serpent form compelld stretch out & up the mysterious
> tree (1982: 356)

The connection is not just an association but an identity, an archetypal metaphor. Formally popular material – again not necessarily British popular literature – prepares the reader for this metaphor. The reader of Yeats, for example, has been primed for this metaphor. For that reader, the ghastly tree in Yeats' 'bitter glass', identifiable with the 'ravens of unresting thought', prefigures the metaphor comprising the 'mysterious tree' and Orc in serpent form.[5]

UK Common-Culture Canon

In chapter 1, I drew attention to the divisive nature of a proliferation of canons. I also spoke warmly of the expanded canon, which incorporates more and more neglected writers into the literary establishment. That is all to the good, but at this point the line of argumentation does point to a supplementary canon: a British, common-culture, literary canon. Quite clearly, such a canon would consist of nothing but middle-strata British literature; it would exclude both the very highbrow and the commercial lowbrow.

It would be imperative that such a canon did not fail to meet the standards of inclusivity vaunted by today's canon reformers. It will be clear by now that this study does not advance the idea that it is only when canons are identity 'matches' for readers that we can begin to take them seriously. The common-culture heritage of a country is *for* all its citizens, regardless of their ethnicity. But, on the grounds of general fairness, canons must evolve as we become aware of their exclusions. That means that it would include not just the British women authors who have been celebrated for decades or hundreds of years, but also other women authors who are newer to canonicity. Of course, included authors must pass muster as 'middle strata', but a number of writers would qualify: Lady Mary Wroth, Margaret Cavendish, Anna Letitia Barbauld, Letitia Elizabeth Landon and many others. Other inclusions would be even more apposite in connection with this study. It would be imperative that middle-strata Scottish, Welsh and Northern Ireland authors are properly represented. Equally important, some middle-strata black writers can be discussed in this British context, especially given the conclusion reached early in chapter 2. In addition to the modern black British writers who can be included in this category (C.L.R. James, James Berry, and so on), the inclusion of earlier black writers who qualify, such as Ignatius Sancho and Olaudah Equiano, would be crucial.

Conclusion

British common-culture literature could be said to consist of two strata of British literature. British literature of the formally popular type, even if it is not necessarily the kind of literature the less well-off habitually consume, represents a literature that everyone, regardless of educational capital, may ultimately enjoy. The upper-middle category is certainly the kind of British literature that requires some level of training on the part of the reader, which might seem to definitively disqualify the common reader. But, as Frye explains, the formally popular is a gateway literature providing the reader with the literary training s/he needs to approach British literature which is highbrow but popular.

5. Common-Culture British Broadcasting

Common-culture British broadcasting is national, which means that it consists of UK productions. But what qualifies as egalitarian British broadcasting? This chapter deals with where we might stumble upon an understanding of radio and television programmes which parallels the one I have spoken of in connection with literature. I explain that one version of the philosophy of public service broadcasting in the UK provides us with just such an understanding – that is, it represents an account of programming which sheds light on what constitutes common culture in this context. Before turning specifically to that account, I will rehearse the understanding of the 'communicative arts' shared by Frye and Hoggart.

Frye and Hoggart on the Communicative Arts

As we have seen, in his work, Frye invokes a conventional distinction between industry and politics, and he identifies leisure as a third sector in society. The fact that culture is flanked by business and politics is highly significant, in the view of both Frye and Hoggart. Crucially, high politics and economy are always ready to dominate the leisure structure.

On one level, the two impact on culture in the forms of the advert and propaganda. On a basic level, these 'genres' may be categorized in connection with whether they respect or fail to respect the integrity of culture. When the advert or the political message *supplements* the film or programme, we can say that the integrity of the work has at least been respected. But, of course, in many cases advertising or propaganda insinuate themselves into the film or programme itself. This can be surgical, as in cases of product placement (legal on UK television since 2011 but not on the BBC), or suffused, as in the case of the propaganda film. With respect to advertising and propaganda which supplement culture, it is striking that in the United Kingdom we have so many commercial adverts and so few paid advertisements by political parties. (In the run-up to an election, there is a window for campaign advertising, but, under normal circumstances, broadcast political messaging is (wisely) prohibited.) Industry enjoys a free hand in this regard.

Of course, today the infiltration of culture by advertising and propaganda has gone supernova, as it were. This is the age of online advertising in relation to consumerism and micro-campaigning in connection with elections, which depends on data harvesting, which, it is increasingly understood, is 'the price' of our use of search engines, social media, etc. The brave new world of the near future looks set to be centred on marvels such as 'smart homes' and the Internet of Things. The idea of phenomena of this type is coming under considerable justified scrutiny. But the tradition of Frye and Hoggart reminds us of the fact that *each and every* intrusion of industry and politics into leisure is undesirable or at best sub-optimal, 'low-tech' intrusions included. After all, it is always something alien to culture which is insinuating itself.

Long before such innovations, Hoggart was given to grousing about the lack of personal integrity in involvement in advertising. Speaking of actors promoting goods they have no real passion for, he observes that

> Some will think it holier than thou to take up an ethical position especially today, when, as we have abundantly seen already, to offer any decision on a judgement of value, is becoming increasingly "not worth making a fuss about". They simply do not see why they should not take the money and buy that weekend cottage in the country. It seems not to occur to them, as they praise foods they have probably not eaten or stores they do not patronize, that they are misusing their voices and faces for gain; and, more, are deceiving many

who have come to admire them for fine acting and may now be tempted to accept what they say without question. (2004: 93)

For his part, in *The Modern Century*, Frye identifies the advert and propaganda as a kind of anti-culture. At the level of language, the problem is rhetoric, understood in a particular way. In *Anatomy of Criticism*, Frye distinguishes between ornamental speech and persuasive speech, commenting that 'Rhetoric has from the beginning meant two things' (2006a: 227). The second of these Frye clearly views as a problem of the modern world. In terms of early discussions of rhetoric, he probably has in mind Plato's *Gorgias*, where, unable to meet Socrates' challenge, Gorgias concedes that rhetoric is the language which allows the ignorant to speak to the ignorant with more powers of persuasion than experts.[1] In *The Modern Century*, Frye also speaks of what he calls 'stupid realism', the visual dimension of modern anti-culture:

By stupid realism I mean what is actually a kind of sentimental idealism, an attempt to present a conventionally attractive or impressive appearance as an actual or attainable reality... We see it in the vacuous pretty-girl faces of advertising, in the clean-limbed athletes of propaganda magazines, in the haughty narcissism of shop-window mannequins, in the heroically transcended woes of soap-opera heroines, in eulogistic accounts of the lives of celebrities, usually those in entertainment, in the creation by Madison Avenue of a wise and kindly father-figure out of some political stooge, and so on. (2003a: 33)

Rhetoric in the sense of persuasive speech is the language component of this audio-visual anti-culture:

What corresponds for the ear to stupid realism in the visual arts is partly rhetoric...the surrounding of an advertised object with emotional and imaginative intensity, the earnest, persuasive voice of the radio commercial, the torrent of prefabricated phrases and clichés in political oratory. (2003a: 36)

We could be forgiven for assuming that Frye takes an equally low view of all mass culture, but we soon discover that he does not. In *The Modern Century*, he identifies a key opposition of the modern world, based on the distinction between a passive and an active response to our surroundings. Having spoken of the self-consciousness of Western culture, he goes on to address this opposition:

On one side are those who struggle for an active and conscious relation to their time, who study what is happening in the world, survey the conditions of life that seem most likely to occur, and try to acquire some sense of what can be done to build up from those conditions a way of life that is at least self-respecting. On the other side are those who adopt a passive and negative attitude, responding to the daily news and similar stimuli, aware of what is going on but making no effort to understand either the underlying causes or the future possibilities. (2003a: 8-9)

Of course, this opposition is clearly another rehearsal of the opposition between contrasting attitudes to culture which we looked at in chapters 2 and 3. Importantly, Frye argues that the arts in the modern world encourage the active response, implicitly critiquing the passive reaction:

The theatre of this conflict in attitudes is formed by the creative and the communicating arts. The creative arts are almost entirely on the active side: they mean nothing, or infinitely less, to a passive response. (2003a: 9)

When considering which kinds of cultural phenomena represent the opposite kind of response, Frye, though he is about to reject it, entertains the idea that mass culture is always met with a passive response:

> The phrase "mass culture" conveys emotional overtones of passivity: it suggests someone eating peanuts at a baseball game, and thereby contrasting himself to someone eating canapés at the opening of a sculpture exhibition. (2003a: 10)

Advertising and propaganda, he concludes, do represent a kind of counter-culture if compared to the arts proper. They are 'on the side' of the other half of this dialectic: 'The words "advertising" and "propaganda" come closest to suggesting a communication deliberately imposed and passively received' (ibid.). Advertising and propaganda are anti-culture, for Frye, although, as we shall see in chapter 6, he advocates a particular 'defence' which is effective against these genres. But Frye, like Hoggart, is of the view that mass culture, is not a domain without value, as its critics say it is. In his thinking, mass culture is redeemed by an active response. Commenting on the two hypothetical audiences he has conjured, he observes that

> The trouble with this picture is that the former is probably part of a better educated audience, in the sense that he is likely to know more about baseball than his counterpart knows about sculpture. Hence his attitude to his chosen area of culture may well be the more active of the two. And just as there can be an active response to mass culture, so there can be passive responses to the highbrow arts. These range from, Why can't the artist make his work mean something to

the ordinary man? to the significant syntax of the student's question, Why is this considered a good poem? (2003a: 9)

Common-culture Broadcasting

Against this backdrop, Frye is interested in how communicative arts such as film and broadcasting can best fulfil their potential. Like Hoggart, he has a sense of a tension between government and leisure, and a preference for what to do in relation to that tension. Both writers advocate that film and TV be turned over to the leisure structure through the creation of institutions such as the BBC and the Film Council (which took over funding responsibilities from the British Film Institute). Under these conditions, film and TV enjoy some freedom from the commercial and political pressures just spoken of. Hoggart states that, in the British context, 'the BBC is trusted to try to be objective, not to be any government's or commercial concern's mouthpiece' (2004: 21). Contrasting the options for Western countries with Marxist states, where 'The complete control of the leisure structure by the political or economic power is a logical development', Frye argues that

> Every effort of a government, however timid, to set up national film and broadcasting companies, and thus to turn over at least some of the mass media to the leisure structure, is part of a fateful revolutionary process...If the growth of the leisure structure is as important and central a development as I think it is, some of the major possibilities of further social development remain with the more industrially advanced democracies. (2003a: 51).

On one level, the dream is that our lives are largely free of advertising and propaganda. This kind of thinking about industry and politics produces in our day the idea that it might be better to pay for search engines as well as social media, although the public appetite for such options appears to be minimal. More radically, Shoshana Zuboff has advocated a complete overhaul of digital, whereby it is put through a revolution paralleling the root-and-branch reform of capitalism in the modern period (see Zuboff, 2018). Developments beginning in 2020 are suggestive of unhappiness about the kind of and amount of propaganda conveyed by digital. One well-known multinational technology company announced restrictions on political ads on its service. Additionally, a well-known microblogging and social networking service declared that it would no longer be possible to pay for political ads. And in the run-up to the 2020 US election an online social media and social networking service began to experiment with moratoria on political ads. (Of course whether such developments have any connection with the kind of attitude to advertising I am rehearsing here is something of a moot point. Critics suggest that such changes to rules may simply amount to a moral panic over deliberately misleading content.)

But this organization of the communicative arts doesn't simply protect us from propagandistic content and adverts; it is also conducive to common culture. Let's narrow the focus to broadcasting, the subject of this chapter. Where the programming is determined by one of the two sectors, particular types of programmes are likely to emerge. Industry is probably more powerful than government in the UK in this regard. (Of course, since 2003, ITV has been beholden to the Contracts Rights Renewal, which means that it must chase ratings or risk losing advertising revenue.) But when production companies, controllers, commissioners, and, where relevant, heads of departments are free of the pressures that can come from advertisers (focused on the holy grail of ratings) something else may emerge.

Of course, the idea of a domain which distributes culture on a level which is somewhat free of the pressures of commercial success might suggest the kind of culture that has little to do with a common culture. It can come off as rather patrician-sounding, and here we return to that challenge. It is a well-known fact that to an extent the BBC still understands its mission in terms of the highbrow Reithian principles set down by its first Director General (to inform, educate and entertain). Broadcasters such as the BBC are so patrician, it could be argued, that they even use a practice known as 'bundling', whereby in order to get the masses to consume programmes that are 'good for them', the BBC bundles them up with popular programmes. The serious programme is sandwiched between the two popular ones: the idea is that people might be tricked into watching something that doesn't reflect their taste. In another patrician iteration, the second Director-General of the BBC, Sir William Hailey, advocated a 'cultural-pyramid' kind of broadcasting system, in which viewers and listeners proceeded up a ladder of broadcasting, until they reached the promised land of the Third Programme.[2]

But another idea typical of PSB thinking and championed by Hoggart provides us with a concept which is more consistent with the provision of common culture.[3] While he is more than ready to criticize bad broadcasting, Hoggart is of the view that UK PSB content has much to commend it. In contrast to Neil Postman's scathing evaluation of US television in the 1980s, Hoggart, without losing his critical edge, sometimes produces ringing endorsements of PSB content in the United Kingdom. He argues – as recently as 2004 – that, along with other PSB channels to a degree, the BBC has in part a broadcasting record it can be proud of:

It would be fair to agree, once again, that British broadcasting in the past and in the present, transmits many admirable programmes, over a very wide spread and all well within the public service remit, and across the terrestrial sound and television channels: news, current affairs, documentaries, drama, sport (probably too much), music, comedy, some situation comedies and much else – though many of the more serious in that list are not now regularly transmitted in prime time. This is true, though to a less balanced degree, of the commercial channels as well as of the BBC. (2004: 133)

Of course, it is a stated aim of PSB that programmes, be they on radio or television, possess universal appeal.[4] And that introduces the perennial issue of social class into the discussion. If Hoggart is of the view that the programming in question doesn't exclude on the grounds of social class, what other characteristics does PSB have?

Crucially, Hoggart also divides programmes into two types tied in with their level of seriousness. On the one hand, we have 'much on Radio 4 and, on television, some programmes on history, the universe and the arts' (2004: 116). In more recent times, content falling into this category would include radio programmes such as *The Media Show*, *Start the Week*, *Great Lives*, and, on television, the latest David Attenborough documentaries, *Civilizations*, etc. But, importantly, a less serious category is also replete with good programming. Hoggart produces a list of entertainment shows which includes the old and the new:

The Goon Show...The Fast Show...Hancock's Half Hour, Morecambe and Wise, Steptoe and Son, Till Death us do Part, Yes, Minister, Dad's Army, Fawlty Towers, One Foot in the Grave, The Office, The Royal Family, The League of Gentlemen. (ibid.)

To which it would be necessary to add everything from *Extras* to *Inside Number 9, W1A, The Thick of It* and *Fleabag*.

At the same time, he posits programme types which are decidedly sub-optimal. Hoggart is of the view that if there is nothing of 'the popular' in the more demanding highbrow programmes, the public service dimension is absent. At the other end of the scale, another stratum of programmes represents the kind of broadcasting which is sub-optimal because, while it is popular, it fails to pass muster as 'good' television or, to a lesser extent, 'good' radio. Bailey *et al* sum up Hoggart's targets in the following manner:

> reality TV or confessional chat-shows, which tempt us with cheap, "peeping-tomery". And quiz shows such as *The Weakest Link*, which compel us to delight in the "dog-eat-dog", humiliation of others. (2011: 156)

Bailey also alludes to the kind of programme taken off the air after the publication of the Pilkington Report – shows such as *Take Your Pick* (2011: 140), mercilessly satirized by *Monty Python* in the sketch 'Spot the Brain Cell'. In our day, unhappiness with this kind of programme has set its sights on programmes such as *The Jeremy Kyle Show*, ultimately taken off-air after a previous guest took his own life.

We are edging towards another four-level understanding. Hoggart commends a simple framework for talking about the optimal and sub-optimal in the context of radio and television. It emerges that the two levels of programmes that he expresses a preference for represent the kind of programming that appeals across classes. He credits one-time BBC executive Huw Wheldon with the all-important insight:

> It may be apt to bring in here another of Wheldon's favourite declarations: that one of public service broadcasters' main aims should be: *"To make good programmes popular and popular programmes good"*. [My emphasis.] That can sound pawky or superior or self-evident. It can also be interpreted as much more weighty and percipient. By "good" programmes he meant those made because the broadcaster thought them,

though perhaps "difficult", of great value and wished without "selling them" by oversimplification to make them widely available. By popular programmes he meant those unlikely to appeal to and not designed specifically for a highly educated audience but which became "good" because they too did not sell out by patronising, or secretly despising, their audience's taste, by talking down to them. (2004: 116)

Wheldon's formulation provides us with a vocabulary for sub-optimal programming as well. If the ideal of Wheldon is that good programmes be popular, and popular programmes good, the danger is that television and radio programming is rather like a parody of the ideal: the good is unpopular, and the popular is bad. Hence:

'Elite'	Good but unpopular
Highbrow and popular (the popular-highbrow)	Good and popular
The favoured popular	Popular but good
The disfavoured popular	Popular but poorly-made

Figure 5

What we have here is a conception of television programmes which parallels the four-level understanding of literature laid out in the previous chapter.[5] Common-culture UK broadcasting consists of the programmes belonging to the two middle strata.

The Future of UK Common-Culture Television

We might bring this chapter to a close by focusing on television. Common-culture literature involves an enormous amount of the literary heritage. By contrast, it is probably the case that, while some heritage television may constitute part of the common-culture television, for the better part, a common-culture TV diet will forever include far more recent television. (Perhaps BritBox will lead to a greater amount of legacy TV consumption.) This means that we continue to need providers who commission, produce and broadcast the two-tier TV culture that I have spoken about. But the implication of this is that traditional pay-TV services as well as subscription video on demand must also unambiguously adopt this attitude to television. It is true that the five UK PSB channels are holding their own.[6] In 2018, their share of broadcast TV rose to 52% from 51% the year before (Ofcom, 2019: 6), and the first sixth months of 2020 saw that share fluctuate between 54.6% and 58.8% (Ofcom, 2020: 19). But if the share of other providers is going to be somewhere close to a half, it is imperative that they adopt the same TV culture as the PSB one.

Given what was said in chapters 2 and 3 about the commercial nature of the disfavoured popular, we shouldn't be surprised if such providers find it difficult to focus on middle-strata culture: after all, they are fully subject to the laws of the marketplace. But it behoves them to make such programming their focus, and the case can easily be made. Common culture depends on it.

Of course, we should not exaggerate the differences between PSB and non-PSB. The BBC should always opt for middle-strata TV culture, secure in the knowledge that such programming is neither elitist nor populist; but it does not always ignore the siren call of good ratings, even if that is the whole point of the licence fee. More importantly, common-culture TV is not alien to non-PSB: the two-tier common culture broadcasting I have been speaking about is quite clearly a moveable feast. Indeed, UK PSB content (BBC content, for example) reappears on well-known streaming services, so even if one is not viewing a PSB channel, one might well be watching PSB content. Additionally, co-operations between streaming and pay television services, on the one hand, and organizations like the BBC, on the other, are also indicative of a common purpose. One of the most telling business ventures of today involves co-productions resulting from collaborations between the BBC and newer providers. Two Brothers Pictures co-produced *Fleabag* with Amazon Studios for BBC Three. *His Dark Materials* is a co-production by one UK production company, Bad Wolf, and an American one, New Line Productions, for BBC One and HBO. (Of course, this means it might just as equally be considered US common-culture. One insider recently made the observation that, with respect to drama, the BBC and HBO truly share a vision.) To an extent, programmes typifying this kind of broadcasting get commissioned by streaming services as well. One well-known streaming service offers examples of the good and popular – the documentary *Our Planet*, by Silverback Films – and the popular and good – *The Crown*, by the UK outfit Left Bank Pictures, which, like Silverback Films, has a proven track record when it comes to UK common-culture programmes.

Of course such international services have no mandate to produce *UK material* in any especially large quantity, and so we should not pin too much hope on such services for our provision of domestic common culture. But it is highly desirable that these other services conform to the culture of PSBs like the BBC. Not least because, in a sense, it helps the BBC, that most maligned (and loved) of broadcasters. The more non-PSB embraces common-culture TV, the more an organization such as the BBC can fulfil its mission – without courting oblivion owing to poor ratings or low standards.

6. The Ethics of Melodrama and British Common Culture

Literature and the *Ochlos*

Central to Frye's political thinking is the opposition between democracy and totalitarianism, the *demos* and the *ochlos*, the people and the mob. Individualism has also cropped up in this discussion: freedom has been defined as the amount of individualism in society, and we might approach the subject of this chapter through Frye's definition of liberalism, which we looked at earlier. Let's look at the same statement and how Frye expands on his point. Liberalism is

> the doctrine that society cannot attain freedom except by individualizing its culture. It is only when the individual is enabled to form an individual synthesis of ideas, beliefs, and tastes that a principle of freedom is established in society, and this alone distinguishes a people from a mob. A mob always has a leader, but a people is a larger human body in which there are no leaders or followers, but only individuals acting as functions of the group. (2003a: 257)

Interestingly, the opposition between the people and the mob reoccurs in Frye's thinking about entertainment, a fact which means we should take a second look at what I am calling the disfavoured popular – specifically in as much as it consists of arts featuring plot and characters. In *The Secular Scripture*, Frye returns to the theme of popular literature (and television) and once more makes it clear that he harbours reservations about a lesser kind of popular culture. But here the context is moral, and Frye is openly contemptuous of the disfavoured popular:

> If by popular literature we mean what a great many people

want or think they want to read when they are compelled to read, or stare at on television when they are not, then we are talking about a packaged commodity which an overproductive economy, whether capitalist or socialist, distributes as it distributes food and medicines, in varying degrees of adulteration. Much of it, in our society, is quite as prurient and brutal as its worst enemy could assert, not because it has to be, but because those who write and sell it think of their readers as a mob rather than a community. In such a social context the two chief elements of romance, love and adventure, become simply lust and bloodlust. As in most melodrama, there is often a certain selfrighteous rationalization of the tone: this is what we're all involved in, whether we like it or not, etc. (2006b: 21-22)

We caught a glimpse of this earlier when dealing with mental attitude. He goes on to say that 'the fact that sex and violence emerge whenever they get a chance does mean that sexuality and violence are central to romance' (2006b: 22), but it is clear that his intention is to alert us to an ethical issue surrounding such popular material.

In sets of observations like the ones we just considered, Frye is attempting to provide a contribution to a concern in English letters about American or, better, pseudo-American, exploitative fiction, which finds expression in everything from Orwell's 'Raffles and Miss Blandish' to Hoggart's The Uses of Literacy. Orwell and Hoggart shared something of a common outlook. Both believed that American mass-market fiction was wandering into an ethical grey area. But both were above-all focused on British imitations of that type of debased American fiction – No Orchids for Miss Blandish by James Hadley Chase, in the case of Orwell, and the British 'sex and violence novelettes' published under names such as 'Hank Janson' in the fifties, in the case of Hoggart.[1] Frye is no doubt thinking of a global market for such material, and, as we see in the above excerpt, he is focused on television programmes as much as literature, but his concern is similar to Hoggart's. The interesting difference – one aspect of Frye's contribution to the discussion – relates to how Frye conceives of the problem. Sex and violence *per se*, Frye is saying, are not exactly the problem. 'Lust and bloodlust', tied in with prurience and brutality, represents a better vocabulary if we are seeking terms for the kinds of conventions we might want to question.

However, the most suggestive feature of what Frye says relates to the idea that some entertainment, melodramatic material in particular, gives the impression that it is made for a mob rather than a *demos*. This is especially apposite in relation to UK common culture, for a number of popular UK television series match this description, in particular, the whodunits of our times, ranging from *Waking the Dead*, *Prime Suspect* and *The Inspector Lynley Mysteries*, to *Rebus*, *Hinterland* and (of course) *Broadchurch*.

That said, in what follows the focus is ultimately not on the issue of (common-culture) material, but on quality of response and common culture. Following Frye's line of argumentation, I will comment on how entertainments of this kind can be redeemed by the right audience response. I'll bring my discussion to a conclusion with a short discussion of *Broadchurch*, although most of it is dedicated to a more theoretical consideration of the nature of this kind of entertainment.

Frye on Melodrama

To pinpoint exactly how Frye thinks of melodrama, we need to turn to the section of the first essay of *Anatomy of Criticism* where his focus is melodramatic literature. He structures his thinking about this area of fiction around the figure of the *pharmakos*, the sacrificial victim or scapegoat, chosen to die for the greater good, though he or she is personally guilty of no crime. Of course, such a figure belongs to history as well as literature, and at a certain point in his discussion, he moves from literature to history. But his primary interest is literary: Frye's focus is *pharmakos* as archetype.

In ironic comedy, Frye comments, we see 'the theme of the driving out of the *pharmakos* from the point of view of society' (2006a: 45). Such stories, Frye argues, invariably turn culprits into victims, owing to the figure cut by society in this kind of fictional material. Speaking of fiction of this type, he states that 'Insisting on the theme of social revenge on an individual, however great a rascal he may be, tends to make him look less involved in guilt and the society more so' (ibid.).

Frye continues his study of the *pharmakos* and ironic comedy by shifting the emphasis to popular fiction, which is part of our concern:

> The fact that we are now in an ironic phase of literature largely accounts for the popularity of the detective story, the formula of how a man-hunter locates a *pharmakos* and gets rid of him. (2006a: 43-44).

The dénouement of a detective story in which the culprit gets their comeuppance may seem right and fitting, but Frye shares a different perspective with us. It is not only that social revenge makes society look guilty. In chapter 4, I explained how, in Frye's view, literature is best understood as displaced myth. The dénouement of such a story reminds us that what we are dealing with is a displaced version of a myth in which punishment is meted out after justice has been *arbitrarily* dispensed:

> we move toward a ritual drama around a corpse in which a wavering finger of social condemnation passes over a group of "suspects" and finally settles on one. The sense of a victim chosen by lot is very strong, for the case against him is only

plausibly manipulated. (2006a: 44)

Writing against the background of the growing popularity of hard-boiled crime fiction, Frye pinpoints the fact that this development signals the merging of such popular fiction with melodrama. And it is melodrama that Frye seems particularly concerned by:

> In the growing brutality of the crime story (a brutality protected by the convention of the form, as it is conventionally impossible that the man-hunter can be mistaken in believing that one of his suspects is a murderer), detection begins to merge with the thriller as one of the forms of melodrama. In melodrama two themes are important: the triumph of moral virtue over villainy, and the consequent idealizing of the moral views assumed to be held by the audience. In the melodrama of the brutal thriller we come as close as it is normally possible for art to come to the pure self-righteousness of the lynching mob. (ibid.)

Frye is clearly of the view that such fictional material habituates people to an overconfident readiness to point the finger at individuals whose guilt is far from established, which may guide how they respond to actual rather than just fictional situations. He goes so far as to float the idea that melodrama and the detective story are 'advance propaganda for the police state, in so far as that represents the regularizing of mob violence' (ibid.). Bernard Crick distinguishes between the 'hate-full mob', the real-world mob, on the one hand, and 'the empty mob', the audience as mob, on the other (Crick 2000): Frye is interested in the capacity for the latter to become identical to the former. Orwell concludes that, in the new American fiction, the implied reader is expected to side with a fictional thug. In Frye's account of melodrama, the implied reader sides with society, which is thuggish.

Frye, however, plays down the threat posed by this kind of literature. The notion of 'play' is fundamental if we are to understand this area of cultural life:

> the element of play is the barrier that separates art from savagery, and playing at human sacrifice seems to be an important theme of ironic comedy. (2006a: 43)

And 'play' characterizes melodrama. Consequently, such material can't be taken seriously, he argues:

> The protecting wall of play is still there. Serious melodrama soon gets entangled with its own pity and fear: the more serious it is, the more likely it is to be looked at ironically by the reader, its pity and fear seen as sentimental drivel and owlish solemnity, respectively. (2006a: 44)

Further reducing the level of concern, Frye also stresses the fact that, even in the area of ironic comedy, literature is characterized less by naive melodrama than parody of it. First, we have 'ironic comedy addressed to the people who can realize that murderous violence is less an attack on a virtuous society by a malignant individual than a symptom of that society's own viciousness' (2006a: 45); second, we have material 'directed at the melodramatic spirit itself, an astonishingly persistent tradition in all comedy in which there is a large ironic admixture' (which tends 'to ridicule and scold an audience assumed to be hankering after sentiment, solemnity, and the triumph of fidelity and approved moral standards') (ibid.); and third, 'the comedy of manners, the portrayal of a chattering-monkey society devoted to snobbery and slander [where] the characters who are opposed to or excluded from the fictional society have the sympathy of the audience' (ibid.). Even the simplest form of melodrama, in Frye's view, is a genre which we should respond to ironically, regardless of how strenuously it apparently demands to be taken seriously.

Frye does much to quell worries the reader may have started to feel in connection with melodrama, but certain features of what he says suggest that a certain menace lingers. After all, melodrama can represent a personalized attack:

> In Aristophanes the irony sometimes edges very close to mob violence because the attacks are personal: one thinks of all the easy laughs he gets, in play after play, at the pederasty of Cleisthenes or the cowardice of Cleonymus. In Aristophanes the word *pharmakos* means simply scoundrel, with no nonsense about it. At the conclusion of *The Clouds*, where the poet seems almost to be summoning a lynching party to go and burn down Socrates' house, we reach the comic counterpart of one of the greatest masterpieces of tragic irony in literature, Plato's *Apology*. (2006a: 43)

Moreover, literature, Frye tells us, has an upper and a lower limit, beyond which it is bordered by experiences at the extremes of the human condition. At the end of the *Paradiso*, Dante has an 'imaginative vision of an eternal world' (2006a: 42-43), which is real. Similarly, at the lower end, we have 'the condition of savagery' associated with both comedy and tragedy: it is 'the world in which comedy consists of inflicting pain on a helpless victim, and tragedy in enduring it' (2006a: 43):

> Ironic comedy brings us to the figure of the scapegoat ritual and the nightmare dream, the human symbol that concentrates our fears and hates. We pass the boundary of art when this symbol becomes existential, as it does in the black man of a lynching, the Jew of a pogrom, the old woman

of a witch hunt, or anyone picked up at random by a mob, like Cinna the poet in *Julius Caesar*. (ibid.)

Most importantly of all, Frye, despite his best efforts to gloss over it, makes it clear that some readers (to which we should add viewers) may take such entertainment seriously. He invokes the two arts we glanced at in an earlier chapter: advertising and propaganda. We have a defence against these genres, Frye observes, and he commends the same defence in relation to melodrama. But his disquisition alerts us to the fact that some members of the audience may take melodrama seriously after all:

Cultivated people go to a melodrama to hiss the villain with an air of condescension: they are making a point of the fact that they cannot take his villainy seriously. We have here a type of irony which exactly corresponds to that of two other major arts of the ironic age, advertising and propaganda. These arts pretend to address themselves seriously to a subliminal audience of cretins, an audience that may not even exist, but which is assumed to be simple-minded enough to accept at their face value the statements made about the purity of a soap or a government's motives. The rest of us, realizing that irony never says precisely what it means, take these arts ironically, or, at least, regard them as a kind of ironic game. Similarly, we read murder stories with a strong sense of the unreality of the villainy involved. (2006a: 44-45)

We start with 'cultivated people', which might suggest its opposite, a lumpen audience. Frye, then, appears to drift towards the conclusion that *no one* responds seriously to the genre. However, at the end of the discussion, it again appears that we have two audiences for this kind of material. 'The rest of us...' suggests that audience for whom advertising, propaganda and melodrama are made *does exist*. A portion of the audience takes such material seriously, something which experience confirms.

The import of this last point is worth exploring. To take such material seriously is to cheer on not just social revenge but the punishment of a figure who may be a scapegoat chosen by lot. Under the conditions of such a response, such material may even represent 'advance propaganda for the police state, in so far as that represents the regularizing of mob violence' (2006a: 44).

Unlike Frye's, my own focus is common culture, but his moral considerations may serve to guide us towards a dimension of common culture. His analysis alerts us to a gulf which may persist in our culture. One part of the culture public responds ironically to such material; another group responds seriously. But a common culture can only be guaranteed through our unanimously agreeing on a single approach to melodrama.

The issue at stake was resolved on the more abstract and general level in chapter 3, and on this more concrete level the preferable option is clear enough: the disciplined and responsible response is decidedly preferable, and here that is the response which demands an ironical, detached engagement. On another level, that ironical response represents a liberal (rather than a populist) response to such fictional material. Either way, it is the only option for a common culture.

Case Study: *Broadchurch*, seasons 1 and 2

One of the most important melodramas of recent times is *Broadchurch*. Season two is especially interesting to discuss in this context. Fundamentally, season one is an example of the typical whodunit. We go through the motions of sizing up each of the suspects for a prolonged period, before that finger of condemnation settles on one. Joe's guilt is established through a flashback, and on one level there is no doubt about his guilt.

But an awareness of the structuring myth determines that we are always aware of the fact that what we are watching is a displaced version of a scapegoat ritual, and that questions about the character's guilt remain.

Interestingly, in season two, the structuring myth comes to the fore. The prosecution fails to secure a conviction in court, and the main characters conclude that they have no alternative but to take the law into their own hands. The drama reaches a climax in the scene in the beach house at the top of the beautiful cliffs of Broadchurch, which was the site of the original crime.

We sense that what we are watching is a scapegoat ritual, and that feeling is strengthened by the nature of the main characters' actual punishment of Joe. He is told to leave Broadchurch on pain of death. Ellie assures him she will kill him if he fails to stay away. 'You think you can banish me?' exclaims Joe. Scapegoating, we remember, amounts to ritualistic sacrifice *or exile* (see, for example, Segal 2005: 369). It is also of great relevance that the scene takes place at the top of a cliff. On one level, this is because it is where the crime took place. But on another level the location is tied in with a suggestion as to how Joe would be killed (should he refuse to leave Broadchurch). Throwing someone from a cliff is thought to be part of the ancient *pharmakos* rite (see, for example, Hughes 2013: 161). Of course, at the start of the scene, Beth suggests one death for Joe: she has counted the knives in the beach house and thought of which would be best to use on him. But the storyline also comes very close to explicitly referencing Joe's being thrown from the cliffs. 'We could kill you here, dump your body on the beach', states Ellie. Even if that kind of execution is not fully explicitly referred to, when such a story is approached in this way, these features get thrown into sharp relief.

From this point of view, the vengeful characters are a mob. The programme is exactly the kind of melodrama Frye speaks of. The problem, clear by now, is a particular kind of response to such material: specifically, the kind of response which takes a programme like this one seriously. Such a response is bereft of what Frye describes as a 'sense of the unreality of the villainy involved' (2006a: 45). It involves emotionally participating in a narrative in which not only is the enemy of society an individual (morally alien to society), but a figure suggestive of an innocent or scapegoat is punished. The alternative response, which treats such fiction as an ironic game, is the only defensible option.

Conclusion

Chapter 2 clarified that even if taste and participation in the United Kingdom were to converge around middle-strata material, a common culture might fail to emerge because of the enormous significance of the mental attitude we adopt to culture. Mental attitudes are potentially so different that we could be left with two cultures after the evolution of a common culture centred on middle-strata taste/participation. That chapter arrived at the conclusion that the only option is to encourage a disciplined and responsible attitude to culture, which could become a common attitude. This chapter has examined a particular area of culture, melodrama, and how two contrasting attitudes can be brought to bear on fictional material of this type, and it has defended the disciplined and responsible attitude in this particular domain.

Epilogue: Two Last Challenges

A New Multiculturalism

I referred earlier to Eric Kaufman's advocacy of a symmetrical multiculturalism, in which whites are encouraged to enjoy their culture in the same way as minorities are invited to preserve their cultural heritage. Let's take a closer look at Kaufman's thesis, giving consideration to the challenge posed by it to my own argument.

With the UK in mind, Kaufman speaks of the moment in the early 2000s when civic identity became more important in connection with the three legs of the 'national stool':

> If the three legs of the national stool consist of the ethnic majority, minorities and common values, there was a transfer of weight from minorities to common values, but no concession to majority identity. (2019: 158)

A new emphasis on common values is inadequate as a solution to the problem of asymmetrical multiculturalism, Kaufman argues, because it fails to grant sufficient importance to majority ethnicity identity. Key for Kaufman is the fact that, across white-majority societies, those majorities are in decline. Not only are common values (rather than majority ethnicity identity) promoted; against the backdrop of such majorities disappearing, governments prove forever less willing to protect the white-majority heritage:

> As the white share of nations declines, a thin, inclusive, values-based nationalism is promoted by governments which sidelines symbols many whites cherish, like Christopher Columbus or Robin Hood. In addition, some minorities challenge aspects of the national narrative like empire or

Western settlement. This lifts the fog for many whites, making them aware of their exclusive ethnic symbols by separating these out from those that are inclusive, like the Statue of Liberty. (2019: 9)

Kaufman's solution involves white majorities enjoying their cultural heritage in a way which parallels how minorities celebrate and preserve theirs. 'We need a new "cultural contract"', he suggests,

> In which everyone gets to have a secure, culturally rich ethnic identity as well as a thin, culturally neutral and future-oriented national identity. Scrubbing the white ethnic stamp from national identities, as governments are attempting to do, is fine, but to do this while suppressing the expression of white identity is problematic. (2019: 535-536)

If the reader has successfully made his or her way through the pages of my own study, the response to Kaufman's ideas will hold no surprises. It is as though Kaufman has focused on one part of the critique of multiculturalism, specifically the fact that it demotes what he terms majority white identity, but disavowed other dimensions, especially how multiculturalism leads to segregation. He throws all the emphasis onto cultural parity without giving commonality its due. In his UK of the future, UK citizens agree on common values but lack other points of contact. Beyond that, they inhabit separate communities. As I suggested earlier, citing Goodhart, to participate in society, is to participate in a common life or conversation, regardless of ethnicity. Something along the lines of Parekh's essentialism seems to influence Kaufman's thought: cultures are to be matched up with ethnicities, and one should limit oneself to the heritage most clearly tied in with one's ethnicity. It is true that on one level 'whiteshift' refers to the process whereby a future mixed-race majority in, for example, the UK might adopt the (largely white, from this point of view) British cultural heritage, which troubles the connection between ethnicity and culture, but even here ethnicity and culture get connected. Membership of the new majority depends on ethnicity: 'Only those with some European background can be members' (2019: 533).

As we evolve our sense of common culture, it becomes clear that there is no need to limit ourselves to the culture that 'goes with' our specific ethnic identities. Rather, we may begin to understand the feasibility of what we might term a rich, common cultural identity, which compliments the 'thin, inclusive, values-based nationalism' Kaufman speaks of. Again, this is not a 'one size fits all' solution; as already explained, the rich cultural identity can exist in different variations. Nor does the culture behind such an identity represent all of a person's culture; we all enjoy the culture of other countries alongside that of our own. To revisit the relevant aspect of my thesis, in spite of the (ethnic) identity which can be attributed to the cultural heritage of a country, such a heritage is *for* everyone – indeed, as suggested, with its universal qualities, it is not only for domestic minorities but everyone everywhere, just as their cultures are also *for* everyone else. Consequently, we may be far more ambitious in our shared identity. People belonging to different ethnic groups, as well as different social classes, can certainly participate in the same culture. We can share far more than institutions and values.

The Implications of Value Judgements

In their outstanding books about the United Kingdom, Larry Elliott and Dan Atkinson advance the important argument that 'the lot' of working people in the UK has been getting steadily worse for decades. The authors' double focus is 'the relaxation of state control over capital and the tightening of state control over individuals' (1999: 208). To focus on the latter, this development now amounts to a 'new authoritarianism' which supplants the previous 'live-and-let-live' attitude (1999: 210). In the first instance, this cultural upheaval was the project of Conservative governments, but New Labour picked up where the Conservatives left off, presenting control culture to the public as 'communitarianism' (1999: 211). In the authors' view, the story of the first decade of the present century involves the working-class suffering at the hands of both neoliberalism and a middle-class Left which has given up on economic reform and turned to 'identity politics and social engineering' (2008: 104). While acknowledging that the British public generally would appear to be the object of all these efforts (2008: 213), the authors emphasize the focus on the working class. Labour 'set itself the task of "restructuring" this unhealthy, malfunctioning section of society without political risk...[a part of New Labour's stance on crime] was a blank cheque for a frontal assault on working-class attitudes and activity' (2008: 213). The authors document how this culture resulted in new jobs being created to make the new controls a reality. Having referenced 'joke jobs' ('outreach coordinators and healthy living strategists', etc. (2008: 107)) and positions in the 'burgeoning equality (or "equalities"...) industry' (ibid.), they comment wryly on 'the expansion of state sector positions not only of dubious utility, to put it mildly, but often actively involved in social engineering projects aimed squarely at members of the traditional working class, whether assaults on their diet or lack of exercise or attempts to change their "attitudes" (or "thoughts", to put it less coyly)' (2008: 108).

Elliott and Atkinson's view is obviously relevant in a study partly about equality in the UK today. And there is a challenge to my line of argumentation here as well – even if the present writer is very much ideologically in sympathy with the duo. The lot of working people, in the view of Elliott and Atkinson, has suffered as a result of the middle-class Left becoming disillusioned with the working class, owing to the burgeoning materialism of that

more common culture and therefore more heritage culture is not necessarily a hopeless cause characterized by the wrong politics. Subscription to this aspiration does not entail sympathy for any of the other measures or policies that Elliott and Atkinson rightly critique. An interest in cultural improvement does not sanction social engineering or the micromanaging of private lives; nor does it justify feelings of contempt for material advancement or legitimize disillusionment felt by a disappointed middle-class Left. Such reactions are anathema to this writer as well.

Appendix: The BBC and Common Culture

Once we have a basic understanding of common culture, and of UK common culture in particular, certain conclusions about a broadcaster such as the BBC suggest themselves. It is uncontroversial to say that the BBC should be a provider of common culture: the idea of public service broadcasting is obviously very close to the idea of common culture. As suggested by the foregoing study, for BBC content to represent common culture two characteristics are essential. Content should be national and it should be middle-strata or egalitarian in that specific sense.

It is easy enough to define what it means for a broadcaster such as the BBC to be national. It means that an enormous amount of its content should consist of programmes (be they radio or television) which are produced in the UK, by British production companies, *from every part of the country*. Earlier, I namechecked a number of such UK production companies: Left Bank Pictures, Silverback Films, Bad Wolf. The BBC itself, as well as its divisions, also produces programmes representing British content. It is necessary that production companies from all over the country are involved in the development of UK broadcast content. The new Director-General of the BBC, Tim Davie, appears to be committed to local and regional broadcasting, even if job losses seem to be in the pipeline

The issue of material which represents middle-strata or egalitarian content points to a more difficult conversation. Adopting a Hoggart-type perspective, in this study, I have conceded that, to an extent, British broadcasting fails to cut the mustard as common culture. Where programming is a) somewhat highbrow and bereft of a popular dimension, or, b) very popular but lacking in terms of the standards of excellence modelled by other programmes: in these cases, broadcasting fails to meet the criteria which are indicative of common culture.

Today, the UK government seems determined to steer the BBC away from common-culture programming. The year 2016 saw the publication of a report commissioned by the Department for Culture, Media and Sport which argues that the BBC should focus on 'distinctive content', not just to preserve its own identity, but to 'make room' for commercial broadcasters and their more popular (sometimes populist) content. But it appears that distinctive content would amount to a diet of upper-strata content (highbrow-and-unpopular as well as popular-highbrow), which would be distinct from a common-culture output.

The chief challenge today, however, is that a rival organizing principle wields too much influence. Much is made of the BBC's bias in its reporting and even in drama and documentaries. On a more fundamental level, too much of its programming also reveals an underlying bias: in terms of the most basic organizing principle, its programming seems to be inordinately influenced by identity politics. This kind of programming aims to provide a multicultural *smorgasbord* for a multicultural society. But such programming is distinct from the kind of programming which is focused on common culture. Rather than thinking of society as a single group consisting of numerous sub-groups all of which are capable of enjoying variations on the same common culture, it provides bespoke content for separate groupings. The corporation has already invested heavily in this idea. As Blair Spowart argues in 'The Public Broadcaster without a Public', the 'BBC has given up on speaking to the public as a whole, on representing a coherent, unified British demos. Now, it implicitly divides its services along age, ethnic and class lines' (Spowart 2015).

The Hoggart-type approach is quite clearly based on class politics rather than identity politics. Class politics sounds like an alternative bias; and so it is, in a sense. But it is worth considering the fact that that bias comes with an enormous advantage: common-culture broadcasting is possible when we allow class politics to inform broadcaster programming.

Each time charter renewal comes around, changes are made to how the BBC is run. Looking forward to 2027 (the time of the next BBC Charter renewal), the common-culture perspective suggests that while some trends should continue, others should change. The BBC should continue to produce, support and broadcast British content. A more radical change of direction may be required in connection with the fact that, as common culture, BBC content should produce egalitarian content. We should undoubtedly define 'egalitarian' in relation to class rather than identity politics when considering what optimal common-culture broadcasting might consist of.

Endnotes

1. National Identity and Cultural Inequality: Challenges in the United Kingdom Today

1. In his *Cosmopolitan Vision*, Beck discusses the 'cosmopolitan outlook', which he compares favourably with the 'national outlook' characterized by social ills such as exclusive identities. Kaufman sees such cosmopolitanism as a kind of white obligation (2019: 341). Of course, in practice it is not only members of white majorities that adopt cosmopolitanism; it is an appealing credo for people from all types of background. Recently, in another study of identity, Appiah advocates cultural cosmopolitanism. Despite his advocacy of the 'liberal state' (2018: 102), Appiah's chief interest is cosmopolitanism, which is underpinned by a sense that, 'you really can walk and talk in a way that's recognizably African-American *and* commune with Immanuel Kant and George Eliot, as well as Bessie Smith and Martin Luther King Jr. No Muslim essense stops individual inhabitants of Dar al-Islam from taking up anything from the Western Civ. syllabus, including democracy. No Western essense is there to stop a New Yorker of any ancestry taking up Islam. Wherever you live in the world, Li Po can be one of your favorite poets, even if you've never been anywhere near China' (2018: 206-207).

2. Ed West labels such multiculturalism 'hard multiculturalism' (2018: 12). In the US, Kronman calls it 'a more destructive version' of multiculturalism (2007: 165).

3. Malik makes the observation that the Parekh report 'has come to be seen as defining the essence of multiculturalism' (2012: 63) in the United Kingdom.

4. Multiculturalism can even be conjoined to nationalism, which is obviously a surprising juxtaposition. After all,

multiculturalism tends to demote or effectively abolish national identity; we might therefore have expected it to prove incompatible with a movement which determinedly sets out to create new national identities. But the emphasis in multiculturalism is a celebration of identities, and nationalism, cultural nationalism especially, is also focused on identity. Moreover, the Scotland and Wales of the future would be multicultural societies. England is trickier, from this viewpoint, but perhaps a new England might also eventually join the family of advanced multicultural nations.

5. Goodhart suggests the first wave of factors consisted of the news coverage of the Sangatte refugee camp, the riots in Bradford, Oldham and Burnley, and, of course, 9/11. Greater emphasis started to be placed on British civic identity in the wake of these events. One report, the Cantle report, which looked into the causes of mill-town riots, floated the idea of both citizenship tests and ceremonies marking the beginning of a new citizen's citizenship. The year 2002 saw the first Life in the United Kingdom tests (citizenship tests), a requirement under the Nationality, Immigration and Asylum Act (2002). Also in 2002, citizenship classes were introduced in UK schools. By 2006, the year after the terror attacks in London, New Labour Prime Minister Tony Blair had taken to exploring the (considerable) limits to multiculturalism in speeches such as the one delivered on 8 December, bearing the title 'The Duty to Integrate: Shared British Values'. Later Gordon Brown aired similar concerns about the UK's asymmetrical multiculturalism. And, subsequently, David Cameron inveighed against what he called 'state multiculturalism' in a speech in Munich in 2011. Interestingly, the story of how hard-line multiculturalism was rejected in the UK could be said to begin with resistance to a particular kind of racialized thinking. When the Parekh

report was published in 2000, the UK political class, along with the mass media, both of whom were sensitive to how the report would be received by the public, baulked at its conclusions. As Kaufman suggests, 'Politicians and the media, receptive to academic ideas but attuned to public sentiment, roundly condemned the more radical findings such as the claim that white exclusivity was built into the term "British"' (2019: 155).

6. Until now, controversy has focused more on specifics such as statues and curricula, rather than integration, but integration may become the focus before long; it is obviously one possible larger context for various foci of protest, and it is implied by much of the critique advanced. Summing up (very neatly) the emerging 'turn', one commentator has spoken of how the cultural Left of today seems hell-bent on introducing its own version of segregation. See Fraser Myers, 'We are sleepwalking into segregation' *spiked online*, 16 July 2020.

7. It might be useful to list the versions of multiculturalism which authors set up in opposition to hard-line multiculturalism and which this study embraces. Goodhart's 'liberal multiculturalism' has already been mentioned. Ed West refers to 'soft multiculturalism' which simply denotes 'cultural interaction' – he also references 'the idea that a society filled with diverse cultural, ethnic and racial groups is in itself a good' (2018: 12), while Fukuyama suggests that, in one respect, multiculturalism simply describes 'societies that [are] de facto diverse' (2019: 111). In the next chapter, I'll turn to Anthony Kronman's definition of the benign version of multiculturalism, which is also highly appealing.

8. 'Region', which I will return to in the next chapter, provides an important type of diversity. Additionally, British culture is by turns conservative and radical, and everything in-between. It also exhibits a variety of religious tendencies,

historically, types of Protestantism and Catholicism, but more recently other kinds. These factors become abundantly clear when we work with British literature, for example.

9. Such an understanding of oppression can only be understood within the context of a larger culture of psychological rather than material injustice. Sacks charts the evolution of the kind of politics in which we do not negotiate improvements in political or economic conditions, but for 'recognition, regard, self-esteem', 'something never before held to be the business of politics' (2007: 55). In Sacks' view, these elements add up to a new way of understanding oppression. 'Marx', he begins, 'had spoken about economic oppression. His latter-day successors speak about psychological oppression: our group underachieves because it is discriminated against, if not explicitly then implicitly. This is an offence against the right of each group to self-esteem. We are the victims, not of a crime, but of a culture. We are the new oppressed' (ibid.). As Sacks and others have commented, this is part of the legacy of the therapeutic turn, analysed in the first instance by Philip Reiff. It has also been discussed in connection with Lasch's concepts of self-esteem and narcissism. As Fukuyama comments while discussing Lasch, 'the promotion of self-esteem enabled not human potential but a crippling narcissism', and narcissism would lead to 'a broad depoliticization of society, in which struggles for social justice were reduced to psychological problems' (2019: 98-99). If this were not bad enough, newer trends, centred on university campuses, produce not knowledge but psychological pressure. Lukianoff and Haidt have written about the mind-set generated by the 'three Great Untruths' (2018: 4), which result in safetyism on university campuses (and beyond). Young people, the authors argue, are being *encouraged* to engage in cognitive distortions, including the kind of 'emotional reasoning'

that leads people away from critical thinking. If it was hyperbolic of Sacks to speak of 'pathological...victimhood' (2007: 53), the idea seems increasingly justifiable today. As Pluckrose and Lindsay put it, speaking of Lukianoff and Haidt's book, various trends in contemporary culture result in 'a kind of reverse cognitive behavioral therapy (CBT)' (2020: 132).

10. Crucially, different sorts of association are suggested by these pluralisms, he argues. The first kind of pluralism is predicated on 'voluntary association' – 'association which springs from an internal act of adherence, from a free act of will' (2001: 201). The latter 'privileges inherited or natural attributes...whether language or ethnic identity, skin colour, sexual orientation or mere geographical location' (2001: 202). In other words, 'the implication of the second form of pluralism is that personal identity and social order are better secured by involuntary forms of association' (ibid.). As writers such as Darcus Howe and Clifford Longley point out, often such 'involuntary' associations do not survive contact with reality: people will also reject their membership of a social group (Longley, 2002: 257) – although the theory, we should say, invariably survives contact with data suggesting rogue non-conformity.

11. Underscoring the relevance of these considerations to multiculturalism, Siedentop gives a concrete example of what he has in mind. By allowing Islamic schools to teach 'the radical subordination of women' (2001: 204), we may be safeguarding the liberty of a group; but we may be sacrificing individual liberty in the process. And the shift to groups may also be self-defeating, he suggests. Siedentop calls multiculturalism an 'apparently hospitable point of view' (2001: 200). But he argues that it is through the ascendancy of liberal version of pluralism that progress has been made. That type of pluralism brings in the possibility of

'Invoking conscience and choice against involuntary forms of association and subordination' (2001: 203) – a gesture which may represent 'the genius of European civilization' (ibid.). It is this form of resistance that has secured the very equalities that the rival form of pluralism aims to champion: it represents 'the moral logic which has brought into question one traditional difference of status and treatment after another, a scrutiny which has cast doubt on whether birth, wealth, gender or even sexual preference are morally relevant grounds for treating people differently' (ibid.).

12. See M. H. Abrams, *A Glossary of Literary Terms*, 31.

13. Already I have adopted a 'haves and have-nots' paradigm, when, of course, the researchers develop a far more sophisticated account of class in their work. Like Guy Standing before them, Savage *et al* suggest that we should think in terms of seven social classes when discussing class in the United Kingdom. And of course, in their schema, it is not the case that the amount of cultural capital groups possess simply becomes less as one moves down the class structure. Generally speaking, that is true, but there are several different kinds of exception to that rule. For example, the traditional working class have higher levels of highbrow cultural capital than the new affluent workers, even though the latter are 'above' them in the class structure (2015: 169). Nonetheless, Savage *et al* do revert to a fairly simple set of contrasts between those who are better off and have more education, on the one hand, and those who are less well-off, on the other, and I adopt the same shorthand in this study. Interestingly, another schema of social class in the UK also invokes the 'haves and have-nots' paradigm. The NRS social grade is a six (or seven) level schema mapping social class. But this framework is often simplified so that a two-level schema comprising ABC1s and C2DEs emerges.

14. Hoggart stops short of dealing with the *attitude* we take to

culture – his focus is on taste and participation – but his message is clear enough. When it comes to culture, value judgements are indispensable.

15. In his US-focused study, Lilla, like Fukuyama, concedes that identity-based movements had a positive impact in several respects in terms of social justice (2017: 77). Additionally, identity politics 'encouraged academic disciplines to widen their scope' (2017: 83). But the problems it brings to US life are legion. Lilla places 'romanticism' at the root of a series of developments; he refers to European roots, and, although he doesn't namecheck its founding fathers, it is clearly Rousseau amongst others he has in mind. Romanticism is confined to artistic romanticism in US life until the 1960s when 'political romanticism' starts to make its presence felt. Lilla argues that this credo might encourage a flight from society to preserve the self; alternatively, it can produce the desire to 'transform society so that it seems like an extension of the self' (2017: 72), an option that Fukuyama emphasizes when speaking of Rousseau-inspired liberalism. Such political romanticism was the guiding ethos of the US New Left, which ushered in a focus on identity. Identity politics, however, tore that political movement apart: without a common identity, such as that of the citizen, groups quickly become aware that other groups in the 'coalition' are also oppressors. They focused on converting the outside world to the pattern of the inner world, so that 'there is no space between what they felt inside and what they did out in the world' (2017: 76). If the New Left had promoted both issue-based politics and identity-based politics, by the 70s, the latter was in the ascendancy. It wrought havoc on our conception of commonality (2017: 78). The universities became the holdout of identity politics, and its creed took over scholarship and studies. Its positive impact on academia was compromised by its 'obsessive fascination

with the margins of society' (2017: 83). For decades now, a humanities education has been an invitation to engage in years of solipsism: the student plumbs the depths of her own being – although what is sanctioned is aspects of her being corresponding to an identity category – moving further and further away from the common *We*. Lilla argues that this conception to identity amounts to 'radical individualism' (2017: 87), and goes on to set up an opposition between citizenship, on the one hand, and the absurdity of the 'Facebook model of identity' (2017: 89). That model of identity promotes a corresponding model of political engagement, which is detrimental to reasoned debate. And if that were not bad enough, it re-introduces taboos (2017: 90-91).

16. The 'direction' in question is similar to that of writers such as Hoggart in his day and Goodhart in ours. Despite his reservations about the concept, Hoggart seems to have harboured an interest in the idea of common culture too. In an interview with John Corner, he begins with scepticism but then pivots to a compelling and sympathetic account of common culture: 'Actually, that phrase was Raymond's much more than mine. I always had some difficulties with it. I rarely used the phrase and was always a bit wary of it. My starting point, my definition of it, was always the separation, the enormous separation between the educated and the rest in this society, and the way in which that very often overlays our common humanity in the sense of common history and traditions. When I used that phrase I would be pointing to, and attempting to recognize, that level of common humanity and history against the appalling divisive forces that are still at work' (Corner 1991: 150). Also of interest are Goodhart's thoughts on integration. He suggests that we understand integration 'in terms of *convergence of life*

chances without convergence of lifestyles', before conceding that 'some lifestyle difference can be an obstacle to life-chance convergence' (71: 2013). He then adds the further caveat that this understanding of integration must be supplemented by what one might call '"lived" integration' (ibid.). He goes on to say, 'The common-sense version of this I have heard several times, from white Britons, is "buying the local paper and supporting the local football team". That is too specific and prescriptive but captures the spirit of it. To put it more abstractly it is about becoming comfortably part of the common life and conversation of wherever you live – and through that the whole country as a whole' (ibid.). His description is a partial match for what I think of as participating in common culture. Of course, there is a second dimension to participation in common culture: the different social classes participate in the 'common life and conversation' as well.

17. John Corner has suggested that 'Hoggart shows himself to be disinclined to work too far outside established and dominant ideas of cultural value and, with moments of exception, outside of established ideas about the "scope for change" within the economic, social and political order' (2011: 70). But Charlie Ellis argues that Hoggart's view of the connections between culture, on the one hand, and politics and economics, on the other, is similar to Crick's (2008: 209). If he is right, Corner's analysis of Hoggart's understanding of culture and society is incomplete.

2. Common Culture as National and Egalitarian Culture

1. It has been observed that while the political Right in many countries today stresses the importance of national identity (frequently defining national identity in exclusive terms), the political Left throws all the emphasis on to diversity and the lack of sharedness. In as much as this is true, Frye's

account of culture provides us with an account of identity which achieves a balance between unity and diversity, and therefore Left and Right.

2. Frye's theory of literature and Van der Merwe's theory of music parallel each other in a remarkable manner. 'During the seventeenth and early eighteenth centuries', writes Van der Merwe, 'the dealings of "serious composers" with popular music had been quite unselfconscious. No one regarded such composers as anything other than highly skilled craftsmen, but, on the other hand, no one questioned the superiority of their product. When it suited them, they used the popular idiom without embarrassment' (204: 132). Similarly, Frye provides us with a history of literature in which serious writers customarily draw on popular literature for inspiration: 'As a rule, popular literature...indicates where the next literary developments are most likely to come from. It was the popular theatre, not humanist neo-Classical drama, that pointed the way to Marlowe and Shakespeare; it was the popular Deloney, not the courtly and aristocratic Sidney, who showed what the major future forms of prose fiction were going to be like; it was the popular ballad and broadside and keepsakebook doggerel of the eighteenth century that anticipated the *Songs of Innocence* and the *Lyrical Ballads*. In prose, the popular literature signalizing such new developments has usually taken the form of a rediscovery of the formulas of romance' (2006b: 23).

3. Interestingly, Van der Merwe argues that modernist music progressively emerges as a non-popular art, but even here he charts the persistence of the popular in twentieth-century art music. The process whereby the popular is expunged from art music is complete by mid-century but the first 4 decades of the century produced modernist music which was also popular, everything from Mahler's Symphony No.

5 to Prokofiev's *Romeo and Juliet*.

4. We should, of course, bear in mind Arendt's warning that while 'there are many authors of the past who have survived centuries of oblivion and neglect…it is still an open question whether they will be able to survive the entertaining version of what they have to say' (2001: 11).

3. Objections and Responses

1. Much of the work done in this field has its intellectual roots in the works of Immanuel Wallerstein, who championed what is known as 'world systems theory', which argues that global systems rather than nation states must be our focus if we are to understand phenomena such as capitalism, environmental crisis, etc.

2. When it comes to how much scope there is for criticism which goes global in this way, Dimock also overeggs the pudding. As Anthony Kronman has argued, most of the 'conversations' involving Western figures are purely Western. As he explains, 'Philo and Augustine grapple with Plato. Hobbes assaults Aristotle. Shakespeare confronts Machiavelli. Spinoza corrects Descartes. Kant answers Hume, Paine condemns Burke, Eliot recalls Dante, Brunelleschi studies the Pantheon, and so on without end' (2007: 167-168).

3. Fukuyama sets up a stark opposition between the two liberalisms. On the one hand, there is the tradition which encapsulates both Kant and the Anglo-American liberal tradition; on the other, we have the liberalism of Rousseau, which Fukuyama disfavours (2019: 52-53).

4. According to Frye, Milton thinks of this higher liberty as the freedom God wants for humanity; humanity itself is nervous about such responsibility: '[L]iberty is the chief thing that the gospel has to bring to man. But man for Milton does not and cannot "naturally" want freedom: he

gets it only because God wants him to have it. What man naturally wants is to collapse back into the master-slave duality, of which the creator-creator duality is perhaps a projection' (2006: 253). The idea of 'original sin' takes on a specific meaning in this context. 'From our present vantage point', observes Frye, 'we can characterize this conception of original sin more precisely as man's fear of freedom and his resentment of the discipline and responsibility that freedom brings' (ibid.).

5. In his iterations of his conception of fraternity, Frye bypasses the nation state (2003a: 57-58). Indeed, one of his most important points is that we should consider fraternity in a post-national context. But when we proceed to the idea of cultural equality and common culture, we have no choice but to re-introduce the nation state, even if that involves our rebutting Frye's cosmopolitanism. The only possible context for genuine common cultures at the present time, after all, is the national context.

6. In a letter to Sister Bettina from 1967, Frye sheds a light on how he worked with Mill's liberalism. 'I think the main influence has been…in following Mill's conception of liberalism into education and society' (2009b: 85), he comments.

7. In terms of creed, Arnold himself was a liberal who became nervous about the reform of his time, which had as its goal a significant extension of the franchise. Despite the fact he was a liberal, he took a great interest in the Oxford movement of the time, which was characterized by political conservatism as well as Anglo-Catholicism. But, in Frye's opinion, a different, less partisan kind of political sensibility is also detectable in *Culture and Anarchy*. Frye contends that Arnold's conception of culture unites something of each class-based political viewpoint. As we have seen, Frye's intention is to associate political values

with different sectors, but he is also sensitive to a level on which culture itself has a connection with all three values. Culture is 'the essence of everything good in conservative, liberal, and radical values': 'It was conservative because it was aware of and accepted its tradition, and because it was a source of social authority. It was liberal because it was held, not through faith or dogma, but through reason and imagination, incorporating a sense of beauty and the virtues of the liberal attitude, including tolerance and suspended judgment...It was radical because its authority was ultimately a spiritual authority, and so its long-run influence was an equalizing one, dissolving the hierarchy of classes by subordinating class conflict to a wider conception of social concern' (2009a: 49).

4. Common-Culture British Literature

1. 'What is "British literature"?' one might ask. The issue of national culture has in the United Kingdom become muddied through its getting mixed up with questions about 'English culture', and more particularly in connection with 'English literature'. The definition of English literature has been through a number of phases. At present, it means 'Anglophone literature' to a great many English literature lecturers in universities. Consequently, the category has been opened up to all manner of important works of literature. Perhaps Scottish literature was always part of 'English literature' in a university context. Many of us have also studied Irish and American literature under the *aegis* of an English literature course. But when the understanding shifts to 'Anglophone literature' not only are doubts about those categories removed; further domains of literary work get drawn in as well. One obvious category is Anglophone writers from ex-colonies. Many of us who have studied English literature have read and taught, say, Nigerian

author Chinua Achebe's *Things Fall Apart*. Today, when studying English literature, one might even read the works of an author with little or no connection to an Anglophone country, so long as that writer originally wrote in English. Hence, it is no surprise to read the works of Denmark's Karen Blixen when studying English literature.

It is almost an optimal solution to define English literature as Anglophone literature; but not quite. When 'English literature' was more tied in with England or Great Britain or the United Kingdom, it might have been unremarkable to have completed a course without studying any Celtic literature. But it would have been customary to have studied not just Anglophone British literature but also some British Latin literature (in translation, no doubt), one obvious example being Thomas More's *Utopia*. Additionally, it would have been customary to have studied some works of Francophone literature, such as *Le Roman de Tristran*, an Anglo-Norman romance written in a twelfth-century dialect of Western France, attributed to Thomas of England. (Thankfully, literary works such as these can still be found in Norton anthologies, although it's hard to imagine they are taught much.)

The focus on Anglophone literature can also exclude other writers. While some exophonic writers' language of choice brings them *into* Anglophone literature (Conrad, Nabokov, even Voltaire), other exophonic writers adopt a language which takes them out of that literature. Samuel Beckett, who wrote many of his works in French, is a case in point.

One can only be struck by the contrast between the difficulty of defining English literature or, more broadly, English culture in an academic setting, on the one hand, and the relative straightforwardness of defining British culture – a national culture – on the other. For we can quickly define what is meant by British culture. Hopefully this will become clear if we focus once more on what is probably the most difficult area to draw boundaries around: literature. What is British literature? Scottish literature (for now at least) is part of British literature. Irish literature is not, although some of the literature of Northern Ireland is. American literature is not. The Anglo-Norman romances I referred to a moment ago are certainly a part of British literature. *Utopia* and other works by British authors in Latin also form part of British literature. The prose fiction of Karen Blixen originally in English is not. Additionally, British culture, in as much as it is verbal culture, is non-Anglophone culture. It is culture in the Celtic languages. It is also Scots literature. Multiculturalism is the object of a critique in chapter one, but in line with the fact that the United Kingdom has been and is a multicultural society in a certain sense, some authors have chosen to write in the language of their larger families and forebears, and that literature is, in one respect, British literature as well.

2. In the Introduction, we first encountered Frye's idea that there is something both particular and universal about literature. It is, of course, the archetypal nature of literature which gives it its universal relevance. It is worth quoting Frye on the universal nature of literature at length: 'If archetypes are communicable symbols, and there is a center of archetypes, we should expect to find, at that center, a group of universal symbols. I do not mean by this phrase that there is any archetypal code book which has been memorized by all human societies without exception. I mean that some symbols are images of things common to all men, and therefore have a communicable power which is potentially unlimited. Such symbols include those of food and drink, of the quest or journey, of light and darkness, and of sexual fulfilment, which would usually take the form of marriage.

It is inadvisable to assume that an Adonis or Oedipus myth is universal, or that certain associations, such as the serpent with the phallus, are universal, because when we discover a group of people who know nothing of such matters, we must assume that they did know and have forgotten, or do know and won't tell, or are not members of the human race. On the other hand, they may be confidently excluded from the human race if they cannot understand the conception of food, and so any symbolism founded on food is universal in the sense of having an indefinitely extensive scope. That is, there are no limits to its intelligibility' (2006a: 110).

3. Interestingly, Frye also contends that, for the better part, that rump of English literature is characterized by specific religious, political and literary sympathies, and that its affinity with the popular stems from those sympathies: the 'combination of Protestant, radical, and Romantic qualities', he observes, 'is frequent enough in English culture to account for the popularity, in every sense, of the products of it' (2005: 301). Frye argues that 'elite' literature, modernist literature in particular, is characterized by a set of opposing religious, political and literary commitments. His conclusion is that in the context of Anglophone letters literary modernism is something of an outlier: 'There has been no lack of Catholic, Tory and Classical elements too, but the tradition dealt with here has been popular enough to give these latter elements something of the quality of a consciously intellectual reaction' (2005: 301).

4. The notion that Romanticism is 'central to the tradition of English literature' is supported, Frye argues, by the feeling that Shakespeare is also central to that tradition, and that his works and English Romanticism share certain features. In 'Blake After Two Centuries', Frye moves towards the conclusion that if we approach English literature in terms of its political, religious and literary features, each of these is

characterized by the tendency 'to take the individual as the primary field or area of operations instead of the interests of society', and Shakespeare is 'the great poetic example of an inductive and practical approach to experience in English culture which is another aspect of its individualism' (2005: 301).

5. It may even be that the training we get from the formally popular equips us for some top-category literature as well. If we begin with myth, the reader's engagement with, say, *Galatea* and 'Ligeia' equip him or her for Shakespeare's *The Winter's Tale*. In that play, Hermione returns to life at the end of the action. She comes back from the dead (Proserpine); a statue of her comes to life (Galatea). Having enjoyed popular literature, the reader is ready for the play. If we adopt an excessively aggressive attitude to literature, insisting forever that anything that is implausible must have some kind of 'natural' explanation, we might find ourselves insisting that she had not died and that rather than a statue, what was revealed was a 'living statue'. But popular literature, introducing us to the mythical, prepares us for all kinds of violations of the canons of plausibility. The student of Shakespeare's play who has absorbed the mythical nature of literature will hopefully investigate the play's meaning without diminishing its mythical structure. Turning to metaphor, the reader's experience of, say, Yeats's 'The Two Trees' equips him or her to engage with Milton's *Paradise Lost*. Two trees figure in Milton's epic: the Tree of Knowledge of Good and Evil (the tree in the 'bitter glass') and the Tree of Life (the 'holy tree'). Perhaps a sound training, afforded by popular literature, might have prompted professional critics to deal properly with the second tree more quickly. Writing in 1966, commentator Ann Grossman lamented the fact that while critics had dealt comprehensively with the former tree in their works,

the Tree of Life had been neglected in critical treatments. Interestingly, in her exposition of the tree's significance, she starts to think about the tree in part as an archetypal metaphor. Working within the tradition established by figures such as Ambrose, Augustine, Bede, Aquinas and John Bale, she reminds us of 'the traditional identification of the Tree of Life with Christ' (1966: 683).

5. Common-Culture British Broadcasting

1. Of course, rhetoric may be benign or even indispensable to the running of the body politic. In another understanding of rhetoric – in Aristotle's *The Art of Rhetoric* – deliberative rhetoric is simply the language leaders use to communicate with citizens. Mark Thompson, however, argues that today rhetoric of the Gorgias-type is in the ascendancy once more, be it in industry or politics: 'Today Gorgias' approach increasingly holds sway, not just in retail marketing, but in realms of public language' (2016: 174). Thompson suggests that Gorgias-type rhetoric amounts to the use of demonstrative rhetoric (praise and blame) rather than deliberative rhetoric in the political sphere, and he goes on to argue that the 'market-speak' which has come to characterize both advertising and political speech is a form of demonstrative rhetoric.

2. Hoggart actually registers considerable respect for Hailey and his ideas in *The Way We Live Now*. The idea of the 'cultural pyramid' has 'dignity and worth' (1995:153).

3. Another defence against populist programming emerged from the Pilkington Report, over which Hoggart, a committee member, exerted great influence. For a comprehensive account of how the report challenged populism, see Petley, 2015. In contrast to the defence, which I outlined in the main body of this chapter, Pilkington emphasizes the notion that, rather than allowing commissioning, scheduling, etc.

to proceed on the assumption that it is possible to divine the exact contours of popular taste, programming should be guided by the principle of providing as much *variety* as possible in programming.

4. That the BBC's content should have universal appeal has been discussed in some theoretical discussions about public service broadcasting such as *The Public Service Idea in British Broadcasting: Main Principles* published by the Broadcasting Research Unit (later, the Broadcasting Research Institute) (see Hoggart 1995: 119).

5. A decade ago, considerations of levels of television programming resulted in a classic stand-off between commentators focused on standards and those focused upon the politics of thinking in terms of levels of television programmes. Scholars such as Jason Jacobs seek to forge ahead with TV aesthetics, with an eye on material that passes muster as art. His viewpoint is evaluative in that it wishes to make distinctions between different kinds of TV. In a piece from 2011, bearing the title 'Television Aesthetics: A Pre-Structuralist Danger?', Matt Hills responds to Jacobs and others in a significant and rhetorically-striking manner. In this piece Hills says that the work of these critics is 'pre-structuralist', as if to suggest that they are as behind the times as, say, pre-moderns. Hills identifies weaknesses or 'avoidances' in their commentaries. He is clearly of the view that Jacobs is a canon-builder, and Hills is an adherent to the notion that canons are dubious ways of engaging with the world of culture. Canon-builders conduct their business as if the past few decades of theory focused on grounds for scepticism *vis-à-vis* canons had not been written, Hills argues. The major theorist Hills name-checks is, unsurprisingly, Bourdieu. He adheres to Bourdieu's view that the bestowing of a positive value judgement upon a type of culture necessarily involves

the judgements of a dominated class, and he draws our attention to the possibility that critics dealing with TV aesthetics may be guilty of this misdemeanour. It should be patently obvious that it is better to think of levels of TV programmes along the lines suggested by Wheldon and Hoggart. That framework allows us to talk of levels of programmes, perhaps conceding that we have two-tier broadcasting, while emphasizing classlessness. 'Everyone should be able to enjoy both levels of programming', etc.

6. Ofcom identifies Channel 5 as a PSB channel. Whether it passes muster as a PSB channel is, of course, a moot point, although Ben Frow has been praised for his transformation of the channel.

6. The Ethics of Melodrama and British Common Culture

1. In *The Uses of Literacy*, which is perhaps less perspicacious in its analysis if compared to Orwell's discussion, Hoggart focuses on the mass culture embodiment of literature, particularly 'Sex novelettes' (1957: 205). In the stories, all sex is violent, and 'there must be violence all the time' (1957: 213); 'it is violent and sexual, but all in a claustrophobic and shut-in way' (ibid.). Crucially, 'it exists in a world in which moral values have become irrelevant': '"forgiveness," "shame", "retribution", and "to be sullied", "to fall" or "to pay" are all concepts outside their moral orbit' (ibid.). 'Crooks' are defeated in the end, but the texture of the writing is bereft of moral reference. When men and women have sex, they do so as 'physical enemies' (1957: 215). The aim of the writing is to make the readers feel 'the flesh and bone of violence' (1957: 217). Gangster fiction, Hoggart admits, 'moves with a crude force as it creates the sadistic situation'; but even here 'it has the life of a cruel cartoon' (1957: 219). Orwell is a precursor to Hoggart and Frye in

this regard, but he also suggests an entirely different type of critical engagement with brutalist entertainment. In his estimation, fiction utterly changed with the publication of *No Orchids for Miss Blandish*. He expresses concern about the trend for fiction in which criminals are idolized. He sees the appearance of Chase's book as evidence of the Americanization of British reading proclivities: 'In America, both in life and fiction, the tendency to tolerate crime, even to admire the criminal so long as he is a success, is very much more marked' (1944: 220). At best, such stories leave the reader in a world of confused morality. The novel betrays 'nihilistic' traits: there is no moral difference between detective and gangster. At worst, it crudely inverts traditional moral categories. Orwell argues that Chase's 'whole theme is the struggle for power and the triumph of the strong over the weak' (1944: 218), and the reader is invited to sympathize with the powerful. Such storytelling may be indicative of an inversion of the underlying myth of Western literature. 'Perhaps the basic myth of the Western world is Jack the Giant-killer, but to be brought up to date this should be renamed Jack the Dwarf-killer' (1944: 222-223), he concludes.

In an interesting contribution to this kind of approach to culture, James Poniewozik argues in his *Audience of One: Donald Trump, Television, and the Fracturing of America* that the past couple of decades have seen the rise of a new kind of media-generated amoralism, which has been ushered in by antihero entertainments (films and TV programmes), reality TV and Twitter.

Bibliography

Abrams, M. H. (2005), *A Glossary of Literary Terms*, Boston: Thomson Wadsworth.

Appiah, K. (2018), *The Lies That Bind: Rethinking Identity*, London: Profile Books.

Arendt, H. (2001), 'The Crisis in Culture', in eds. J. Nedelsky and R. Beiner, *Judgement, Imagination, and Politics: Themes from Kant and Arendt*, 3-25, Oxford: Rowman & Littlefield.

Arnold, M. ([1869] 2006), *Culture and Anarchy*, Oxford: Oxford University Press.

Ashcroft, B. (2013), 'Globalization, Transnation and Utopia', in eds. W. Goebel and S. Schabio, *Locating Transnational Identities*, 13-29, London: Routledge.

Bailey, M., B. Clarke and J. Walton (2011), *Understanding Richard Hoggart*, London: John Wiley & Sons.

Bennett, T., M. Savage, E. Silva, A. Warde, M. Gayo-Cal and D. Wright (2009), *Culture, Class, Distinction*, London: Routledge.

Best, S. (2007), 'Cultural Turn', in G. Ritzer (ed.), *Blackwell Encyclopedia of Sociology*, 177.

Blackshaw, T. (2013), 'Two Sociologists: Pierre Bourdieu and Zymunt Bauman', in T. Blackshaw (ed.), *Routledge Handbook of Leisure Studies*, 164-178, New York: Routledge.

Blake, W. (1982), *The Complete Poetry and Prose of William Blake*, ed. D. Erdman, Berkley: University of Calfornia Press.

Borde, R. and E. Chaumeton, ([1955] 2002), *A Panorama of American Film Noir, 1941–1953*, trans. Paul Hammond, San Francisco: City Lights Books.

Bradbury, M. (1976), 'The Cities of Modernism', in M. Bradbury and James McFarlane (eds) *Modernism, 1890-1930*, 96-104, London: Penguin Books.

Brick, H. (2000), *Age of Contradiction: American Thought and Culture in the 1960s*, Ithaca: Cornell University Press.

"British Social Attitudes 30" (2013), London: NatCen Social Research. Accessed 20 September 2020. https://www.bsa.natcen.ac.uk/latest-report/british-social-attitudes-30/devolution/trends-in-national-identity.aspx

Collins, J. (2002), 'High-Pop: An Introduction', in J. Collins (ed.) *High-Pop: Making Culture into Popular Entertainment*, 1-31, Malden: Blackwell Publishers.

Corner, J. (1991), 'Studying Culture – reflections and assessments. An Interview with Richard Hoggart', *Media, Culture and Society*, 13 (2), London: Sage.

Corner, J. (2011), 'Confronting Value: A Note', in eds. M. Bailey and M. Eagleton, *Richard Hoggart: Culture and Critique*, 63-74, Nottingham: CCC Press.

Crawford, R. (1992), *Devolving English Literature*, London: Clarendon Press.

Crick, B. (2000), 'Big Brother Belittled', *The Guardian*, 19 August. Available online: https://www.theguardian.com/comment/story/0,3604,356134,00.html (accessed 25 April 2020).

Crow. T. (1996), *Modern Art in the Common Culture*, New Haven: Yale University Press.

Dimock, W. (2003), 'Planetary Time and Global Transition: "Context" in Literary Studies', *Common Knowledge*, Vol. 9, Issue 3, Fall: 488-507.

Elliott, L. and D. Atkinson (1999), *The Age of Insecurity*, London: Verso Books.

Elliott, L. and D. Atkinson (2008), *The Gods That Failed*, London: The Bodley Head Ltd.

Ellis, C. (2008), 'Relativism and Reaction: Richard Hoggart and Conservatism', in S. Owen (ed.), *Richard Hoggart and Cultural Studies*, 198-212, London: Palgrave Macmillan.

Fiedler, L. (1975), 'Cross the Border – Close That Gap: Postmodernism', in M. Cunliffe, (ed.), *History of Literature in the English Language*, Vol. 9 *American Literature Since 1900*. London: Sphere Books. pp. 344-366.

Finkielkraut, A. (1988), *The Undoing of Thought*, New York: Claridge.

Frank, T. (2002), *One Market Under God*, London: Vintage.

Frye, N. (2000a), *Northrop Frye On Religion*, eds A. Lee and J. Grady, Toronto: University of Toronto Press.

Frye, N. (2000b), *Northrop Frye's Writings on Education*, eds J. Grady and G. French, Toronto: University of Toronto Press.

Frye, N. (2002), *Northrop Frye on Literature and Society, 1936-1989*, ed. R. Denham, Toronto: University of Toronto Press.

Frye, N. (2003a), *Northrop Frye on Modern Culture*, ed. J. Gorak, Toronto: University of Toronto Press.

Frye, N. (2003b), *Northrop Frye on Canada*, eds J. O'Grady and D. Staines, Toronto: University of Toronto Press.

Frye, N. (2004), *Fearful Symmetry: A Study of William Blake*, ed. N. Halmi, Toronto: University of Toronto Press.

Frye, N. (2005), *Northrop Frye on Milton and Blake*, ed. A. Esterhammer, Toronto: University of Toronto Press.

Frye, N. (2006a), *Anatomy of Criticism: Four Essays*, ed. R. Denham, Toronto: University of Toronto Press.

Frye, N. (2006b): *'The Secular Scripture' and Other Writings on Critical Theory: 1976 – 1991*, eds J. Adamson and J. Wilson. Toronto: University of Toronto Press.

Frye, N. (2009a): *The Critical Path and Other Writings on Critical Theory, 1963-1975,* eds E. Kushner and J. O'Grady, Toronto: University of Toronto Press.

Frye, N. (2009b), *Northrop Frye: Selected Letters, 1934-1991*, ed. R. D. Denham, New York: McFarland and Company.

Fukuyama, F. ([1992] 2012), *The End of History and the Last Man*, London: Penguin.

Fukuyama, F. (2019), *Identity: Contemporary Identity Politics and the Struggle for Recognition*, London: Profile Books.

Goodhart, D. (2013), *The British Dream: Successes and Failures of Post-war Immigration*, London: Atlantic Books.

Goodhart, D. (2014), 'A Postliberal Future?', *Demos Quarterly*,

Issue 1, winter 2013/2014.

Graham, B. (2011), *The Necessary Unity of Opposites: The Dialectical Thinking of Northrop Frye*, Toronto: University of Toronto Press.

Graham, B. (2013), 'Northrop Frye and the *Opposition* between Popular Literature and Bestsellers', *Academic Quarter*, Vol. 7: 93–104.

Graham, B. (2015), 'Northrop Frye on Leisure as Activity', *Academic Quarter*, Vol. 11, No. 4: 35–46.

Graham, B. (2015), 'Frye and Hoggart on Film and TV: An Alternative to the Postmodernist Paradigm', *Hamilton Arts & Letters*, Vol. 7, No. 2. (n.p.)

Graham, B. (2018), 'The Anti-Elitist Nature of Northrop Frye's Conceptions of Highbrow and Popular Literature', *Philologie im Netz*, 84: 1-18.

Grossman, A. (1966): 'The Use of the Tree of Life in *Paradise Lost*', *The Journal of English and Germanic Philology*, Vol. 65, No. 4: 680–687.

Hamilton, A.C. (1999) 'Northrop Frye as a Cultural Theorist', in D. Boyd and I. Salusinsky (eds), *Rereading Frye: The Published and Unpublished Works*, 103-121, Toronto: University of Toronto Press.

Haslam, N. (2016), 'Concept creep. Psychology's expanding concepts of harm and pathology', *Psychological Inquiry*, 27 (1), 1-17.

Hills, M. (2005), 'Who wants to be a fan of Who Wants To Be A Millionaire? Scholarly television criticism, 'popular aesthetics' and academic tastes', in C. Johnson and R. Turnock (eds), *Independent Television Over Fifty Years*, 177-195, Maidenhead: Open University Press.

Hills, M. (2011) 'Television Aesthetics: A Pre-Structuralist Danger?', *Journal of British Cinema and Television*, 8:1: 99-117.

Hoggart, R. (1957), *The Uses of Literacy*, London: Chatto and Windus.

Hoggart, R. (1972), *Only Connect: On Culture and Communication*, London: Chatto and Windus.

Hoggart, R. (1995). *The Way We Live Now*, London: Pimlico.

Hoggart, R. (2004), *Mass Media in a Mass Society*, London: Continuum.

Hume, M. (2012), *There Is No Such Thing As a Free Press...And We Need One More Than Ever*, Exeter: Imprint Academic.

Hughes, D. (2013), *Human Sacrifice in Ancient Greece*, London: Routledge.

Hunter, I.Q. and Kaye, H. (1997), 'Introduction – Trash Aesthetics: Popular Culture and its Audience', in D. Cartmell, I.Q. Hunter, H. Kaye, and I. Whelehan, (eds), *Trash Aesthetics: Popular Culture and Its Audience*, pp. 1-13, Chicago: Pluto Press.

Jacobs, J. (2001), 'Issues of judgment and value in television studies', *International Journal of Cultural Studies*, 4: 4: 427-47.

Jacobs, J. (2006), 'Television Aesthetics: An Infantile Disorder', *Journal of British Cinema and Television*, 3: 1: 19-33.

Kaufman, E. (2019), *Whiteshift: Populism, Immigration and the Future of White Majorities*, London: Penguin Books.

Kaufman, E. (2020), 'The Rebirth of the Left-Conservative Tradition', *Tablet* (June 16).

Kern R. and R. Peterson, (2016), 'Changing Highbrow Taste: From Snob to Omnivore', *American Sociological Review*, Vol. 61, No. 5 (Oct., 1996): 900-907.

Kronman, A. (2007), *Education's End: Why Our Colleges and Universities Have Given Up on the Meaning of Life*, New Haven: Yale University Press.

Kundera, M. (1995) *Testaments Betrayed*, London: HarperCollins.

Lasch, C. (1991), *The True and Only Heaven: Progress and Its Critics*, New York: WW. Norton & Company.

Leavis, F.R., and D. Thompson (1933), *Culture and Environment*, London: Chatto and Windus.

Leavis, F.R. and D. Thompson (1977), *Culture and Environment*,

Westport, CT: Greenwood Press.

Lilla, M. (2017), *The Once and Future Liberal: After Identity Politics*, New York: HarperCollins.

Lukianoff, G. and Haidt, J. (2018), *The Coddling of the American Mind: How Good Intentions and Bad Ideas Are Setting Up A Generation for Failure*, New York: Penguin Press.

McChesney, R. (1996), 'Is There Any Hope for Cultural Studies', *Monthly Review* (March).

Malik, K. (2012), *From Fatwa to Jihad: How the World Changed*, New York: Atlantic Books.

Matthews, W. (2013), *The New Left, National Identity, and the Break-up of Britain*, Leiden: BRILL

Menand, L. (2011), Introduction to *Masscult and Midcult: Essays Against the American Grain* by Dwight McDonald, vii-xxii, New York: New York Review of Books.

McGuigan, J. (1992), *Cultural Populism*, London: Routledge.

Myers, F. (2020), 'We are sleepwalking into segregation', *spiked online*, 16 July. Available online: https://www.spiked-online.com/2020/07/16/we-are-sleepwalking-into-segregation/ (accessed 10th October 2020).

Müller, J. (2017), *What is Populism?* London: Penguin Books.

Ofcom (2019), *Media Nations: UK 2019*. https://www.ofcom.org.uk/__data/assets/pdf_file/0019/160714/media-nations-2019-uk-report.pdf

Ofcom (2020), *Media Nations 2020 UK Report* https://www.ofcom.org.uk/__data/assets/pdf_file/0010/200503/media-nations-2020-uk-report.pdf

Orwell, G. (1968), 'Raffles and Miss Blandish', in S. Orwell and I. Angus (eds), *The Collected Essays, Journalism and Letters of George Orwell*, Vol. III, 212-224, London: Secker and Warburg.

Parekh, B. (2000), Report of the Commission on the Future of Multi-Ethnic Britain, *The Future of Multi-Ethnic Britain*, London: Profile Books.

Parekh, B. (2002), *Rethinking Multiculturalism: Cultural Diversity and Political Theory*, Boston: Harvard University Press.

Petley, J. (2015), 'Hoggart and Pilkington: Populism and Public Service Broadcasting' in *The International Journal of Communication Ethics*, 12: 1: 4-14.

Pluckrose, H. and J. Lindsay (2020), *Cynical Theories: How Universities Made Everything about Race, Gender, and Identity – and Why This Harms Everybody*, London: Swift Press.

Prince, T. (2012), *Culture Wars in British Literature: Multiculturalism and National Identity*, London: McFarland & Company, Inc.

Sacks, J. (2005), 'Jonathan Sacks: Society is not a house or a hotel it should be a home' (*sic.*), *The Independent*, 31 May. Available online: https://www.independent.co.uk/voices/commentators/jonathan-sacks-society-is-not-a-house-or-a-hotel-it-should-be-a-home-223850.html (accessed 25 April 2020).

Sacks, J. (2007), *The Home We Build Together: Recreating Society*, London: Continuum Books.

Sandoval, M. (2013), 'Participation (Un)Limited: Social Media and the Prospects of a Common Culture', in T. Miller (ed.), *The Routledge Companion to Global Popular Culture*, 66-76, London: Routledge.

Savage, M., N. Cunningham, F. Devine, S. Friedman, D. Laurison, L- McKenzie, A. Miles, H. Snee, and P. Wakeling (2015), *Social Class in the 21st Century*, London: Pelican Books.

Segal, R. (2005), 'Myth and Ritual', in J. Hinnills (ed.) *The Routledge Companion to the Study of Religion*, 356- 378, London: Routledge.

Siedentop, L. (2001), *Democracy in Europe*, London: Penguin Books.

Sontag, S. (1996), *Against Interpretation, and Other Essays*, New York: Dell.

Spowart, B. (2015), 'The Public Broadcaster without a Public', *spiked online*, 15 July. https://www.spiked-online.com/2015/07/15/the-public-broadcaster-without-a-public/

(accessed 20th November 2019).

Standing, G. (2019), *Plunder of the Commons: A Manifesto for Sharing Public Wealth*, London: Penguin, Random House.

Storey, J. (2015), *Cultural Theory and Popular Culture*, New York: Routledge.

Thompson, M. (2017), *Enough Said: What's Gone Wrong with the Language of Politics?* London: Vintage.

Van Der Merwe, P. (2012), *Roots of the Classical: The Popular Origins of Western Music*, Oxford: Oxford University Press.

Williams, R. ([1967] 2014), 'The Idea of a Common Culture', in J. McGuigan (ed.) *Raymond Williams on Culture and Society*, 93-100, London: Sage.

Willis, P. (1990), *Common Culture*, Buckingham: Open University Press.

Willoquet-Maricondi, P. and M. Alemany-Galway (2008), 'A Postmodern /Poststructuralist Cinema', in P. Willoquet-Maricondi and M. Alemany-Galway (eds) *Peter Greenaway's Postmodern /Poststructuralist Cinema*, xiii-xxxv, Lanham: Scarecrow Press, Inc.

Zuboff, S. (2019), *The Age of Surveillance Capitalism: The Fight for a Human Future at the New Frontier of Power*, New York: Public Affairs.

A Call for Contributions

On a Common Culture has as its goal the advancement of a discussion about the possibility of common culture in the United Kingdom today. A large number of important issues are raised by the study, but a great deal of further investigation is also suggested by it. To that end, this call invites contributions for a follow-up volume, which adds to and expands on the material gathered in this first volume.

Submissions may focus on the nature of UK common culture in the various areas not covered in *On a Common Culture*. It is observed in the study that chapter 2 tees up three categories of more specific discussions: commentary about the nature of the national dimension of common culture in connection with specific areas of culture; discussions about the egalitarian or cross-class characteristic of common culture *vis-à-vis* specific arts; and considerations, in specific contexts, of the significance of the idea that our response to common culture should always be responsible and disciplined. Contributions connected to all three categories are welcome. What, for example, are the defining features of 'middle-strata' culture in domains such as music, film, visual arts, newspapers, video games, etc.? Chapter 6 explores one specific aspect of the disciplined and responsible mental attitude integral to common culture, but in which other respects might such an attitude be important to common culture? What of the meaning of such an approach *vis-à-vis* digital communications, for example?

Submissions of a more theoretical nature are also welcome. Chapter 2 of *On a Common Culture* also alludes to the fact that it may be fruitful to study *variations* on common culture tied in with diverse social identities. With respect to those considerations, how might a variation connected to northern England differ from a metropolitan variation, for example? What of common-culture variations relating to other social identities: women, the BAME community, *LGBTQ+*, men, etc.? Of course, there is a danger that such variations lead to new hierarchies, so the most important question to consider here is 'How do we make sure that variations don't result in hierarchies?' Essentially, when do variations speak to dominant and subordinate identities and what characteristics should be added to common culture in order to forestall the development of other aspects of cultural inequality?

Abstracts, approximately 350 words in length, must be submitted by 31 December 2022 to editor Brian Russell Graham. (briang@hum.ku.dk/bg.msc@cbs.dk)

CULTURE, SOCIETY & POLITICS

The modern world is at an impasse. Disasters scroll across our smartphone screens and we're invited to like, follow or upvote, but critical thinking is harder and harder to find. Rather than connecting us in common struggle and debate, the internet has sped up and deepened a long-standing process of alienation and atomization. Zer0 Books wants to work against this trend. With critical theory as our jumping off point, we aim to publish books that make our readers uncomfortable. We want to move beyond received opinions.

Zer0 Books is on the left and wants to reinvent the left. We are sick of the injustice, the suffering and the stupidity that defines both our political and cultural world, and we aim to find a new foundation for a new struggle.

If this book has helped you to clarify an idea, solve a problem or extend your knowledge, you may want to check out our online content as well. Look for Zer0 Books: Advancing Conversations in the iTunes directory and for our Zer0 Books YouTube channel.

Popular videos include:

Žižek and the Double Blackmain

The Intellectual Dark Web is a Bad Sign

Can there be an Anti-SJW Left?

Answering Jordan Peterson on Marxism

Follow us on Facebook
at https://www.facebook.com/ZeroBooks and Twitter at
https://twitter.com/Zer0Books

Bestsellers from Zer0 Books include:

Give Them An Argument
Logic for the Left
Ben Burgis
Many serious leftists have learned to distrust talk of logic. This is
a serious mistake.
Paperback: 978-1-78904-210-8 ebook: 978-1-78904-211-5

Poor but Sexy
Culture Clashes in Europe East and West
Agata Pyzik
How the East stayed East and the West stayed West.
Paperback: 978-1-78099-394-2 ebook: 978-1-78099-395-9

An Anthropology of Nothing in Particular
Martin Demant Frederiksen
A journey into the social lives of meaninglessness.
Paperback: 978-1-78535-699-5 ebook: 978-1-78535-700-8

In the Dust of This Planet
Horror of Philosophy vol. 1
Eugene Thacker
In the first of a series of three books on the Horror of Philosophy,
In the Dust of This Planet offers the genre of horror as a way of
thinking about the unthinkable.
Paperback: 978-1-84694-676-9 ebook: 978-1-78099-010-1

The End of Oulipo?
An Attempt to Exhaust a Movement
Lauren Elkin, Veronica Esposito
Paperback: 978-1-78099-655-4 ebook: 978-1-78099-656-1

Capitalist Realism
Is There No Alternative?
Mark Fisher
An analysis of the ways in which capitalism has presented itself
as the only realistic political-economic system.
Paperback: 978-1-84694-317-1 ebook: 978-1-78099-734-6

Rebel Rebel
Chris O'Leary
David Bowie: every single song. Everything you want to know,
everything you didn't know.
Paperback: 978-1-78099-244-0 ebook: 978-1-78099-713-1

Kill All Normies
Angela Nagle
Online culture wars from 4chan and Tumblr to Trump.
Paperback: 978-1- 78535-543-1 ebook: 978-1-78535-544-8

Cartographies of the Absolute
Alberto Toscano, Jeff Kinkle
An aesthetics of the economy for the twenty-first century.
Paperback: 978-1-78099-275-4 ebook: 978-1-78279-973-3

Malign Velocities
Accelerationism and Capitalism
Benjamin Noys
Long listed for the Bread and Roses Prize 2015, *Malign Velocities*
argues against the need for speed, tracking acceleration
as the symptom of the ongoing crises of capitalism.
Paperback: 978-1-78279-300-7 ebook: 978-1-78279-299-4

Meat Market
Female Flesh under Capitalism
Laurie Penny
A feminist dissection of women's bodies as the fleshy fulcrum of
capitalist cannibalism, whereby women are both consumers and
consumed.
Paperback: 978-1-84694-521-2 ebook: 978-1-84694-782-7

Babbling Corpse
Vaporwave and the Commodification of Ghosts
Grafton Tanner
Paperback: 978-1-78279-759-3 ebook: 978-1-78279-760-9

New Work New Culture
Work we want and a culture that strengthens us
Frithjoff Bergmann
A serious alternative for mankind and the planet.
Paperback: 978-1-78904-064-7 ebook: 978-1-78904-065-4

Romeo and Juliet in Palestine
Teaching Under Occupation
Tom Sperlinger
Life in the West Bank, the nature of pedagogy and the role of a
university under occupation.
Paperback: 978-1-78279-637-4 ebook: 978-1-78279-636-7

Ghosts of My Life
Writings on Depression, Hauntology and Lost Futures
Mark Fisher
Paperback: 978-1-78099-226-6 ebook: 978-1-78279-624-4

Sweetening the Pill
or How We Got Hooked on Hormonal Birth Control
Holly Grigg-Spall
Has contraception liberated or oppressed women?
Sweetening the Pill breaks the silence on the dark side of hormonal
contraception.
Paperback: 978-1-78099-607-3 ebook: 978-1-78099-608-0

Why Are We The Good Guys?
Reclaiming Your Mind from the Delusions of Propaganda
David Cromwell
A provocative challenge to the standard ideology that Western
power is a benevolent force in the world.
Paperback: 978-1-78099-365-2 ebook: 978-1-78099-366-9

The Writing on the Wall
On the Decomposition of Capitalism and its Critics
Anselm Jappe, Alastair Hemmens
A new approach to the meaning of social emancipation.
Paperback: 978-1-78535-581-3 ebook: 978-1-78535-582-0

Enjoying It
Candy Crush and Capitalism
Alfie Bown
A study of enjoyment and of the enjoyment of studying. Bown
asks what enjoyment says about us and what we say about
enjoyment, and why.
Paperback: 978-1-78535-155-6 ebook: 978-1-78535-156-3

Color, Facture, Art and Design
Iona Singh
This materialist definition of fine-art develops guidelines for
architecture, design, cultural-studies and ultimately social
change.
Paperback: 978-1-78099-629-5 ebook: 978-1-78099-630-1

Neglected or Misunderstood
The Radical Feminism of Shulamith Firestone
Victoria Margree
An interrogation of issues surrounding gender, biology,
sexuality, work and technology, and the ways in which our
imaginations continue to be in thrall to ideologies of maternity
and the nuclear family.
Paperback: 978-1-78535-539-4 ebook: 978-1-78535-540-0

How to Dismantle the NHS in 10 Easy Steps (Second Edition)
Youssef El-Gingihy
The story of how your NHS was sold off and why you will have
to buy private health insurance soon. A new expanded second
edition with chapters on junior doctors' strikes and government
blueprints for US-style healthcare.
Paperback: 978-1-78904-178-1 ebook: 978-1-78904-179-8

Digesting Recipes
The Art of Culinary Notation
Susannah Worth
A recipe is an instruction, the imperative tone of the expert, but
this constraint can offer its own kind of potential. A recipe need
not be a domestic trap but might instead offer escape – something
to fantasise about or aspire to.
Paperback: 978-1-78279-860-6 ebook: 978-1-78279-859-0

Most titles are published in paperback and as an ebook.
Paperbacks are available in traditional bookshops. Both print and
ebook formats are available online.
Follow us on Facebook
at https://www.facebook.com/ZeroBooks
and Twitter at https://twitter.com/Zer0Books